OPEN DOOR TO SPANISH

A Conversation Course for Beginners

Third Edition

LEVEL 1

Margarita Madrigal

PEARSON

Prentice Hall

Upper Saddle River, New Jersey 07458

Library of Congress Cataloging-in-Publication Data

MADRIGAL, MARGARITA.

    Open Door to Spanish: a conversation course for beginners. Level 1 / MARGARITA MADRIGAL. —3rd ed.
      p. cm.
    Includes index.
    ISBN 0-13-111611-8
    1. Spanish language—Conversation and phrase books—English. I. Title.

PC4121.M24   2003
468.3'421—dc21   2003048663

Publisher: Phil Miller
Senior Acquisitions Editor: Bob Hemmer
Assistant Director of Production: Mary Rottino
Editorial/Production Supervision: Nancy Stevenson
Executive Marketing Manager: Eileen Bernadette Moran
Assistant Editor: Meriel Martínez Moctezuma
Editorial Assistant: Pete Ramsey
Assistant Manager, Prepress and Manufacturing: Mary Ann Gloriande
Prepress and Manufacturing Buyer: Brian Mackey
Full-Service Project Management: Victory Productions, Inc.

Credits appear on p. 240, which constitutes a continuation of the copyright page.

© 2004, 1995, 1987 by Pearson Education, Inc.
Upper Saddle River, NJ 07458

Printed in the United States of America

10 9 8 7 6 5 4 3 2 1

ISBN   0-13-111611-8

Pearson Education LTD., *London*
Pearson Education Australia PTY, Limited, *Sydney*
Pearson Education Singapore, Pte. Ltd.
Pearson Education North Asia Ltd., *Hong Kong*
Pearson Education, Canada, Ltd., *Toronto*
Pearson Educación de Mexico, S.A. de C.V.
Pearson Education—Japan, *Tokyo*
Pearson Education Malaysia, Pte. Ltd.
Pearson Education, *Upper Saddle River*, New Jersey

PREFACE

INTRODUCTION

The *Third Edition* of **Open Door to Spanish** and the accompanying cassettes have been thoroughly updated and revised, and are appropriate for classroom use or for self-instruction. After completing both levels of the program, users can look forward to conducting simple conversations successfully in Spanish as well as understanding many advertisements and articles written in Spanish. Even a rudimentary knowledge of Spanish can be important when applying for a job. Applicants with an ability to understand more than one language are often given preference for jobs in medicine, social work, tourism, government, and other businesses.

APPROACH

Margarita Madrigal's books have been used by thousands of students around the world. Former successful students applaud the *Madrigal Method*: its simplicity, its copious use of cognates, and its humor. The conversations, explanations, exercises, activities, and tapes in **Open Door to Spanish** teach students to recognize the large number of words and expressions that are alike in English and in Spanish (cognates), strategies and rules for converting English words to Spanish, hints for identifying large numbers of new words in Spanish, and formulas to help students use Spanish verbs to describe events in the past, present, and future.

Students report extraordinary retention rates and the human quality of instructors adopting Margarita's approach. The many conversations in **Open Door to Spanish** reflect what people say every day on the streets, in restaurants and cafes, on the phone, or at home with friends and family. Spanish is fun!

ACKNOWLEDGMENTS

Margarita Madrigal passed away several years ago after touching the lives of many people. She developed the methods used in **Open Door to Spanish** while teaching Spanish in New York. She taught celebrities, politicians, and ordinary people, and gladly stayed after class with students experiencing difficulties. Margarita traveled extensively through Spanish-speaking countries, first as a child with her missionary father and mother, and later as an adult, absorbing the cultures and histories of many countries. Through her teaching and traveling experiences, she learned firsthand about the methods that work best for learning a new language.

We hope the revised edition rings true to Margarita's voice. We gratefully acknowledge the contribution of Kris Swanson, without whom this *Third Edition* would have been impossible.

Margarita would have been delighted to know the number of schools and students that continue to use **Open Door to Spanish**. Many instructors and students responded to our questions regarding this revision and told us to keep things simple—it ain't broke, so don't fix it. We especially acknowledge and thank Palma Urdiales, Anthony Di Ruzzo, Lula Keyes, Rosita Martínez, Ana Caldero, Diana Cochran, Monika Ecsedy-Nagy, Lisa Nalbone, and the students at Valencia Community College for their suggestions and comments.

Learning a new language can change your life. Take your time! Be patient! Enjoy your introduction to a new language and culture. It may change your life in ways you cannot imagine now.

TABLE OF CONTENTS

SPANISH PRONUNCIATION

VOWELS

A	Like English *art*.
E	Like English *take*, but without the English diphthong.
I	Like English *meet*, but without the English diphthong.
O	Like English *obey*, but without the English diphthong.
U	Like English *too*, but without the English diphthong.

CONSONANTS

B, D, G	Like their English equivalents, *boy*, *dog*, *goat*. After vowels, however, these sounds "soften". **B** becomes closer to the English "v"; **D** becomes like English "th"; and **G** becomes like the French "r" in *Français*.
V	Represents exactly the same sound as Spanish **B**.
F	Like English *fork*.
P, T, hard **C***	Like their English equivalents, *pet*, *toy*, *cake*, but without the aspiration or puff of air which accompanies the English sounds. (A lighted match will go out when the English "p" is pronounced, it will not go out after the Spanish "p".)
S, Z (soft **C**)	Like English *ceiling*.
R	Similar to the English flap in *Betty*, *Teddy*, *Buddy*.
RR	No English equivalent. A trill—like two to three **R**s in rapid succession.
N, M	Like English *no*, *mow*.
Ñ	Similar to English *onion*, *canyon*.
L	Like English clear "l" in *leaf*, not like the dark "l" in *feel*.
LL, Y	Represents same sound. Pronunciation varies widely across regions—it can sound like English *yet*, English *judge*, or French *Jean*. Some varieties may distinguish the two sounds: **LL** like Italian *gli*, and **Y** as above.
J	Like English *loch* or German *ich*.
H	This letter is never pronounced in Spanish.

The hard **C** is also spelled "qu" in Spanish. There is no letter **K** in Spanish.

RULES FOR STRESS AND ACCENT

1. Words ending in a vowel, **n** or **s** are stressed on the next-to-the-last syllable:

   c<u>la</u>se   ha<u>blan</u>do   <u>ca</u>sa   <u>chi</u>cos   <u>tie</u>nen
   <u>co</u>mo   <u>ca</u>si

2. Words ending in a consonant other than **n** or **s** are stressed on the last syllable:

   espa<u>ñol</u>   a<u>zul</u>   me<u>jor</u>   liber<u>tad</u>   mo<u>tor</u>
   fe<u>liz</u>   e<u>dad</u>   com<u>prar</u>   and all infinitives

3. Words which are not pronounced according to the above rules have a written accent on the vowel of the stressed syllable:

   ha<u>bló</u>   estu<u>dié</u>   a<u>sí</u>   di<u>fí</u>cil   <u>lás</u>tima
   pi<u>rá</u>mide   sen<u>té</u>monos   se<u>gún</u>

4. The accent is also used to distinguish words which are spelled alike, but have different meanings or uses:

   él   *he*   el   *the*
   sí   *yes*   si   *if*
   cómo   *how*   como   *as, like*

5. The accent is used to show that a weak vowel (i, u) next to a strong vowel (a, e, o) is stressed:

   d<u>í</u>a   o<u>í</u>do   ba<u>ú</u>l   env<u>í</u>o

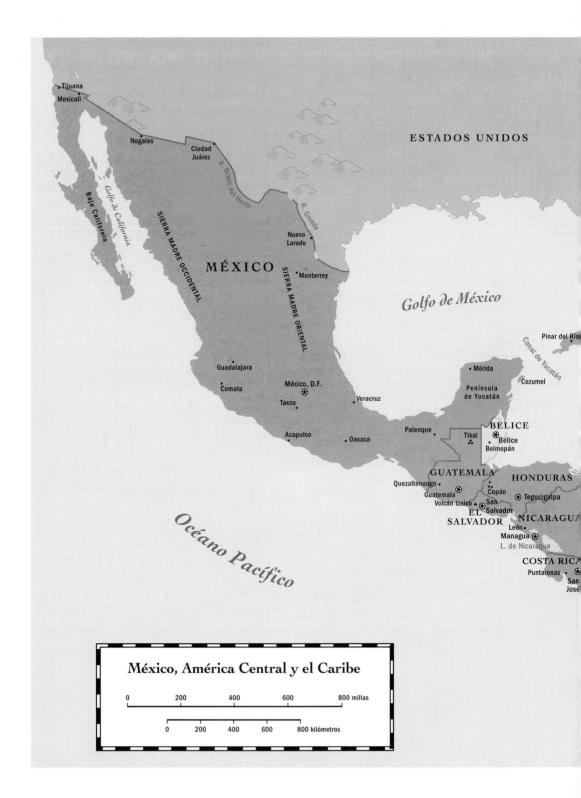

ESTADOS UNIDOS

Tijuana
Mexicali

Nogales

Ciudad
Juárez

R. Bravo del Norte

R. Grande

Golfo de California

Baja California

SIERRA MADRE OCCIDENTAL

MÉXICO

SIERRA MADRE ORIENTAL

Nuevo
Laredo

Monterrey

Golfo de México

Pinar del Río

Canal de Yucatán

Mérida

Cozumel

Península
de Yucatán

Guadalajara

Comala

México, D.F.

Taxco

Veracruz

Acapulco

Oaxaca

Palenque

Tikal

BELICE

Belice
Belmopán

GUATEMALA

HONDURAS

Quezaltenango

Guatemala

Volcán Izalco

Copán

San
Salvador

EL
SALVADOR

Tegucigalpa

NICARAGUA

León

Managua

L. de Nicaragua

COSTA RICA

Puntarenas

San
José

Océano Pacífico

México, América Central y el Caribe

0   200   400   600   800 millas

0   200   400   600   800 kilómetros

x

Océano Atlántico

Estrecho de la Florida

Las Bahamas

Matanzas
La Habana
Cienfuegos
CUBA
Camagüey
Guantánamo
Santiago
de Cuba

REPÚBLICA
DOMINICANA

PUERTO
RICO

HAITÍ
Port-au-Prince
Santo
Domingo
Mayagüez
Ponce
San
Juan
Islas Vírgenes
Antigua

Kingston
JAMAICA

Guadalupe
Dominica

Martinica
Santa Lucía

San
Vicente
Barbados

Granada

Antillas Menores

Mar Caribe

Aruba
Curaçao
Bonaire
Isla
Margarita
Trinidad y Tobago
Port-of-Spain

Caracas

Canal de
Panamá
Colón
Panamá
PANAMÁ
Golfo
de
Panamá

R. Orinoco

VENEZUELA
GUYANA
SURINAM

R. Magdalena

COLOMBIA
Bogotá

BRASIL

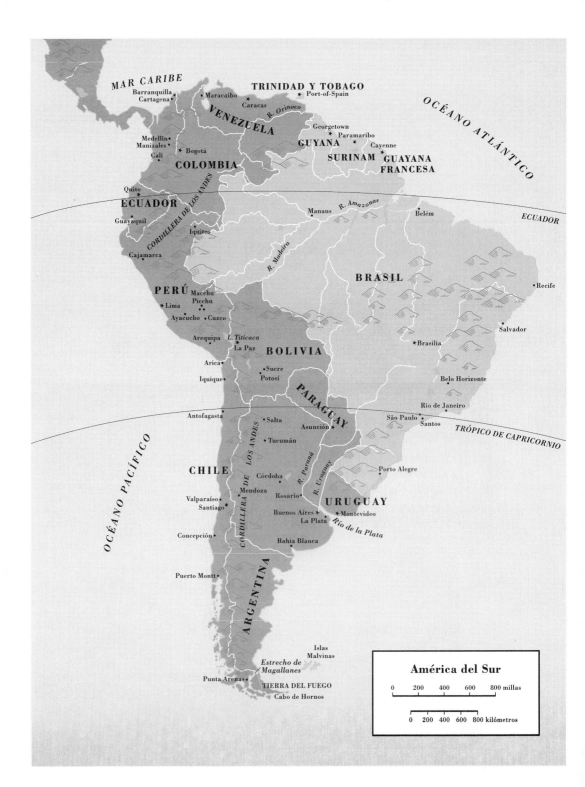

América del Sur

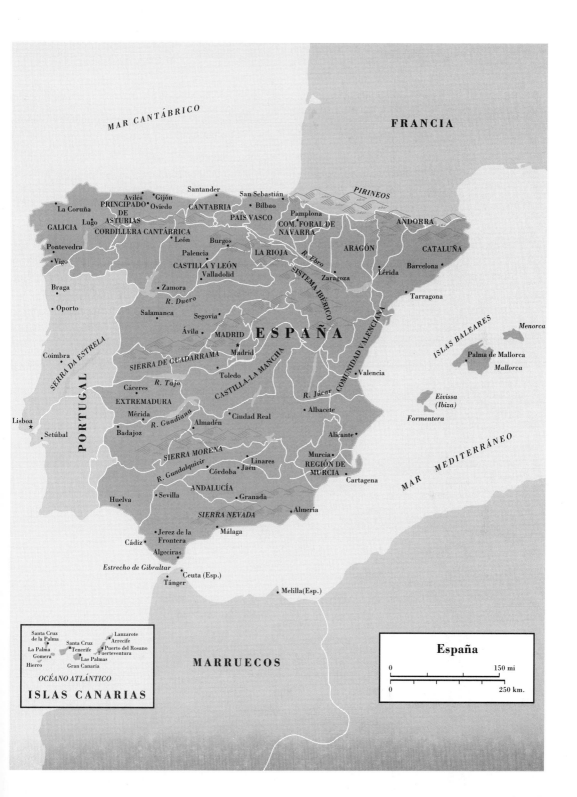

MAR CANTÁBRICO

FRANCIA

PIRINEOS

Santander
San Sebastián
La Coruña
Avilés Gijón
PRINCIPADO Oviedo
DE
ASTURIAS
GALICIA Lugo
CORDILLÉRA CANTÁBRICA
CANTABRIA
PAÍS VASCO
Bilbao
Pamplona
COM. FORAL DE
NAVARRA
ANDORRA
Pontevedra
León
Burgos
LA RIOJA
ARAGÓN
CATALUÑA
Vigo
Palencia
R. Ebro
Barcelona
Braga
CASTILLA Y LEÓN
Valladolid
SISTEMA IBÉRICO
Zaragoza
Lérida
Oporto
Zamora
R. Duero
Tarragona
Salamanca
Segovia
ISLAS BALEARES
Menorca
Coimbra
Ávila
MADRID
ESPAÑA
Palma de Mallorca
SERRA DA ESTRELA
SIERRA DE GUADÁRRAMA
Madrid
COMUNIDAD VALENCIANA
Mallorca
Toledo
CASTILLA-LA MANCHA
Valencia
Eivissa
(Ibiza)
Cáceres
R. Tajo
R. Júcar
EXTREMADURA
Mérida
R. Guadiana
Almadén
Ciudad Real
Albacete
Formentera
Lisboa
Setúbal
Badajoz
Alicante
MAR MEDITERRÁNEO
SIERRA MORENA
R. Guadalquivir
Linares
Córdoba Jaén
Murcia
REGIÓN DE
MURCIA
Huelva
Sevilla
ANDALUCÍA
Granada
Cartagena
SIERRA NEVADA
Almería
Jerez de la
Frontera
Málaga
Cádiz
Algeciras
Estrecho de Gibraltar
Ceuta (Esp.)
Tánger
Melilla(Esp.)

MARRUECOS

Santa Cruz
de la Palma
La Palma
Gomera
Hierro
Santa Cruz
Tenerife
Lanzarote
Arrecife
Puerto del Rosano
Fuerteventura
Las Palmas
Gran Canaria

OCÉANO ATLÁNTICO
ISLAS CANARIAS

España

0   150 mi
0   250 km.

LESSON 1

✳

En el restaurante

- Similar words in English and Spanish (cognates)
- Sentence formation
- **-or** words in Spanish
- Ordering food in a restaurant

1.1 THE CITY AND THE COUNTRY

HOTEL PARADOR

el	*the*	el hotel	*hotel*
el tractor	*tractor*	el sombrero	*hat*
el radio	*radio*	es	*is*
el tren	*train*	el mosquito	*mosquito*
el piano	*piano*	chiquito(a)	*tiny, little*
el plato	*plate, dish*	grande	*big (masc., fem.)*
el disco	*compact*	el rancho	*ranch*
compacto	*disc*	sí	*yes*
el avión	*airplane*		

Pronunciation

1. The letter **h** is always silent in Spanish. The Spanish word hotel is pronounced o-.   2. Notice that there is an accent on the **o** in the word **avión**. Whenever you see an accent in Spanish, stress the accented letter.
3. **Qui** is always pronounced **kee**, as in **keep**.

1.2 LISTENING EXERCISE

Repeat each sentence after your instructor says it, reading along in the book as you speak.

1. El tren es grande.
2. El mosquito es chiquito.
3. El radio es chiquito.
4. El sombrero es chiquito.
5. El tractor es grande.
6. El piano es grande.
7. El plato es chiquito.
8. El disco compacto es chiquito.
9. El hotel es grande.
10. El avión es grande.

Can you do this exercise with your book closed?

1.3 REVIEW—MINI-TEST

Close your book and write the words your instructor says in Spanish.

1. the ranch
2. little

3. the hotel
4. the airplane

5. the train
6. big
7. is

8. the plate
9. the radio
10. the compact disc

Punctuation: Questions

In Spanish, we use an inverted question mark (¿) before questions.

EXAMPLES: **¿Qué es?** *What is it?* **¿Qué es esto?** *What is this?*

1.4 ORAL EXERCISE

Answer the questions with the responses provided.

EXAMPLE: **¿Es grande el tren?** *Is the train big?*
ANSWER: **Sí, el tren es grande.** *Yes, the train is big.*

1. ¿Es grande el tren?
    Sí, el tren es grande.
2. ¿Es chiquito el mosquito?
    Sí, el mosquito es chiquito.
3. ¿Es chiquito el sombrero?
    Sí, el sombrero es chiquito.
4. ¿Es grande el avión?
    Sí, el avión es grande.
5. ¿Es grande el hotel?
    Sí, el hotel es grande.

6. ¿Es grande el piano?
    Sí, el piano es grande.
7. ¿Es chiquito el plato?
    Sí, el plato es chiquito.
8. ¿Es chiquito el radio?
    Sí, el radio es chiquito.
9. ¿Es grande el rancho?
    Sí, el rancho es grande.
10. ¿Es chiquito el disco compacto?
    Sí, el disco compacto es chiquito.

Can you do this exercise with your book closed?

1.5 WORD BUILDER

Pronunciation: Changing English words that end in **-or** into Spanish

Most English words that end in -or are similar to Spanish words. These -or words are easy because you don't have to learn them, you already know them. Practice their Spanish pronunciation. Be sure to stress the last syllable of these words, like this: **mo-TOR**.

List of **-or** words in Spanish (optional)

el actor	el horror	el reflector
el candor	el humor	el rumor
el color	el inferior	el superior
el director	el instructor	el tenor
el doctor	el interior	el terror
el error	el inventor	el tractor
el exterior	el motor	el vapor
el favor	el profesor	el vigor
el honor	el protector	

Note: Spanish words never have a double **s**. For example, the English word *professor* is spelled **profesor** in Spanish.

1.6 REVIEW–MINI-TEST

Close your book and write the words your instructor says in Spanish.

1. the tractor
2. the color
3. the actor
4. the error
5. the motor
6. the doctor
7. the favor
8. the honor
9. the director
10. the humor
11. the vigor
12. the exterior

1.7 EVERYDAY EXPRESSIONS

Buenos días

Buenas tardes

Buenas noches

por favor	*please*	**Bien.**	*Fine.*
pronto	*quickly, soon*	**Buenos días.**	*Good morning.*
pronto, por favor	*quickly, please*	**Buenas tardes.**	*Good afternoon.*
		Buenas noches.	*Good night. Good evening.*
pronto, pronto, por favor	*quickly, quickly, please*	**¿Cómo está usted?**	*How are you? (formal)*
Gracias.	*Thank you.*		
De nada.	*You're welcome.*	**¿Cómo estás?**	*How are you? (fam.)*

1. 8 ORAL EXERCISE

What would you say in the following situations? Choose from the everyday expressions you just learned.

1. You greet someone at 10:00 in the morning.
2. You meet your professor and want to know how she is today.
3. You see your classmate and want to know how he is today.
4. You are buying coffee and you are in a hurry.
5. The counter person hands you your coffee.
6. You greet someone at 10:00 at night.
7. You greet someone at 1:00 in the afternoon.
8. Your roommate thanks you for bringing her a cup of coffee.

1.9 CONVERSATION VOCABULARY

uvas

sopa

café

fresas

el café	*coffee*	la uva	*grape*
el te	*tea*	el rosbif	*roast beef*
el chocolate	*chocolate*	el bistec	*beefsteak*
la sopa	*soup*	Sí, señor.	*Yes, sir.*
el chile con carne	*chili with meat*	Sí, señora.	*Yes, ma' am.*
la fresa	*strawberry*	Sí, señorita.	*Yes, miss.*

¿Hay…? *Is there any…?/Are there any…?*

Pronunciation

Remember that the letter **h** is always silent in Spanish. The word **hay** is pronounced like the word *eye* in English.

 ## 1.10 LISTENING EXERCISE

Repeat each sentence after your instructor says it, reading along in the book as you speak.

1. ¿Hay café?
2. ¿Hay té?
3. ¿Hay rosbif?
4. ¿Hay bistec?
5. ¿Hay uvas?
6. ¿Hay chocolate?
7. ¿Hay fresas?
8. ¿Hay sopa?

1.11 CONVERSATION

Señor and señora López have invited Robert and Mary to a restaurant, where they are placing their orders. Role play their conversation by forming groups of five students each. One student will play the waiter/waitress. The others will play the four customers. Each group will act out the restaurant scene for the class.

Sample order

SRA. LÓPEZ:	¿Hay fresas? Are there any strawberries?
WAITER/WAITRESS:	Sí, señora. Yes, ma'am.
SRA. LÓPEZ:	Fresas, por favor. Strawberries, please.

The following block will serve as a guide for your conversation. However, do not restrict yourself only to what is in the block.

Order anything you want, but only if you can say it in Spanish. Don't forget to greet the waiter/waitress and use courtesy expressions when appropriate.

Ordering in a restaurant

MARY:	¿Hay rosbif?
WAITER/WAITRESS:	Sí, señorita.
MARY:	Rosbif, por favor.
ROBERT:	¿Hay bistec?
WAITER/WAITRESS:	Sí, señor.
ROBERT:	Bistec, por favor.
SRA. LÓPEZ:	¿Hay chocolate?
WAITER/WAITRESS:	Sí, señora.
SRA. LÓPEZ:	Chocolate, por favor.
SR. LÓPEZ:	¿Hay sopa?
WAITER/WAITRESS:	Sí, señor.
SR. LÓPEZ:	Sopa, por favor.

En el restaurante

Study tips

If you want to make rapid progress, learn every word and every rule in each lesson, and practice speaking Spanish on your own.

Study the lists of vocabulary (words you must learn to use) and optional vocabulary (words you should recognize and may want to use) at the end of each chapter. Try to participate frequently in class. The more Spanish you speak, the more quickly you will learn it.

1.12 READING EXERCISE: EN EL RESTAURANTE "LOS PLATOS"

Although you are just beginning your study of Spanish, you've already learned that many English and Spanish words look alike. By focusing on these words, called cognates, you can read more Spanish than you might think. Look at the following menu for the Mexican restaurant Los Platos, and then answer the questions below.

Restaurante Los Platos

Calle Hernández Macías 72, 415/2-24-75, San Miguel de Allende

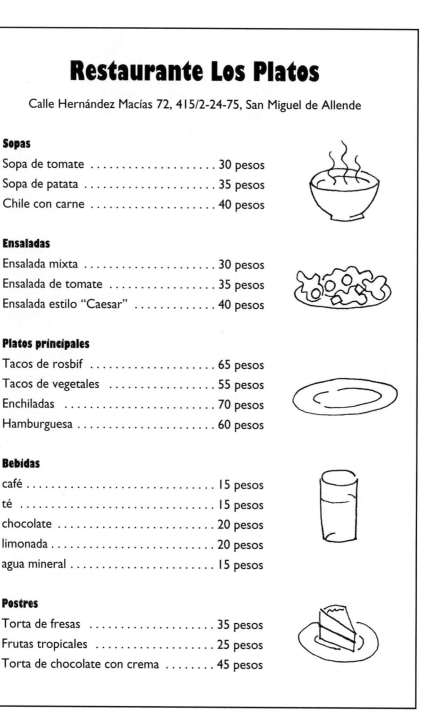

Sopas

Sopa de tomate . . . . 30 pesos
Sopa de patata . . . . 35 pesos
Chile con carne . . . . 40 pesos

Ensaladas

Ensalada mixta . . . . 30 pesos
Ensalada de tomate . . . . 35 pesos
Ensalada estilo "Caesar" . . . . 40 pesos

Platos principales

Tacos de rosbif . . . . 65 pesos
Tacos de vegetales . . . . 55 pesos
Enchiladas . . . . 70 pesos
Hamburguesa . . . . 60 pesos

Bebidas

café . . . . 15 pesos
té . . . . 15 pesos
chocolate . . . . 20 pesos
limonada . . . . 20 pesos
agua mineral . . . . 15 pesos

Postres

Torta de fresas . . . . 35 pesos
Frutas tropicales . . . . 25 pesos
Torta de chocolate con crema . . . . 45 pesos

Now answer the following questions in Spanish, based on the information in the menu.

1. ¿Hay burritos?
2. ¿Hay sopas?
3. ¿Hay enchiladas?
4. ¿Hay pizza?
5. ¿Hay café?

6. ¿Hay tacos?
7. ¿Hay pasta?
8. ¿Hay platos vegetarianos?
9. ¿Hay hamburguesas?
10. ¿Hay chalupas?

1.13 WRITING EXERCISE

Now use the menu for Los Platos restaurant and write a conversation similar to the ones on page 8 of this chapter. Include three people who are customers and the waiter or waitress.

VOCABULARY

NOUNS

el avión	*plane*	el piano	*piano*
el bistec	*beefsteak*	el plato	*plate, dish*
el café	*coffee*	el radio	*radio*
el chile con carne	*chili with meat*	el rancho	*ranch*
		el rosbif	*roast beef*
el chocolate	*chocolate, hot chocolate*	el sombrero	*hat*
		la sopa	*soup*
el disco compacto	*compact disc*	el té	*tea*
		el tractor	*tractor*
la fresa	*strawberry*	el tren	*train*
el hotel	*hotel*	la uva	*grape*
el mosquito	*mosquito*		

ADJECTIVES

chiquito(a)	*little, tiny*
grande	*big (masc., fem.)*

OTHER WORDS AND EXPRESSIONS

Bien.	*Fine.*	**Gracias.**	*Thank you.*
Buenos días.	*Good morning.*	**¿Hay...?**	*Is (Are) there any...?*
Buenas tardes.	*Good afternoon.*	**por favor**	*please*
Buenas noches.	*Good night.*	**pronto**	*quickly, soon*
	Good evening.	**pronto, por favor**	*quickly, please*
¿Cómo está	*How are you?*	**pronto, pronto,**	*quickly, quickly,*
usted?	*(formal)*	**por favor**	*please*
¿Cómo estás?	*How are you?*	**sí**	*yes*
	(fam.)	**Sí, señor.**	*Yes, sir.*
De nada.	*You're welcome.*	**Sí, señora.**	*Yes, ma'am.*
el (la)	*the*	**Sí, señorita.**	*Yes, miss.*
es	*is*		

OPTIONAL LIST

NOUNS

el actor	el inventor
el candor	el motor
el color	el profesor
el director	el protector
el doctor	el reflector
el error	el rumor
el favor	el tenor
el honor	el terror
el humor	el vapor
el horror	el vigor
el instructor	

ADJECTIVES

exterior
inferior
interior
superior

LESSON 2

✸

Lugares de interés
- Negatives
- Definite and indefinite articles (masculine)
- **-al** words in Spanish
- **del**
- Ordering food in a restaurant

2.1 GOING PLACES

es	*is*	el restaurante	*restaurant*
no es	*is not, isn't*	el elefante	*elephant*
el parque	*park*	popular	*popular (masc., fem.)*
el queso	*cheese*	muy grande	*very big (masc., fem.)*
el auto	*car*	muy chiquito(a)	*very little*
el autobús	*bus*	chiquitito(a)	*very, very little; tiny*

Pronunciation

Que is always pronounced **ke**, as in **kept**. **Parque** is pronounced **parke**, and **queso** is pronounced **keso**. **¿Qué?** (*What?*) is pronounced **ke** as in **kept**.

 ## 2.2 LISTENING EXERCISE

Repeat each sentence after your instructor says it reading along in the book as you speak.

1. El elefante es grande.
2. El elefante no es chiquito.
3. El mosquito es chiquito.
4. El mosquito no es grande.
5. El tren es grande.
6. El tren no es chiquito.
7. El avión es grande.
8. El avión no es chiquito.
9. El rancho es grande.
10. El rancho no es chiquito.
11. El plato es chiquito.
12. El plato no es grande.
13. El tractor no es chiquito.
14. El tractor es grande.

2.3 ORAL EXERCISE

Answer the questions with the responses provided.

EXAMPLE: **¿Es chiquito el auto?**
ANSWER: **No, el auto no es chiquito.**

1. ¿Es grande el auto? Sí, el auto es grande.
2. ¿Es chiquito el autobús? No, el autobús no es chiquito.
3. ¿Es grande el autobús? Sí, el autobús es muy grande.
4. ¿Es chiquito el restaurante? No, el restaurante no es chiquito.
5. ¿Es grande el elefante? Sí, el elefante es muy grande.

6. ¿Es chiquito el hotel? No, el hotel no es chiquito.

7. ¿Es chiquito el tren? No, el tren no es chiquito.

8. ¿Es chiquito el avión? No, el avión no es chiquito.

9. ¿Es chiquito el mosquito? Sí, el mosquito es muy chiquito.

10. ¿Es chiquito el parque? No, el parque no es chiquito.

11. ¿Es grande el queso? No, el queso no es grande.

Can you do this exercise with your book closed?

2.4 REVIEW–MINI-TEST

Close your book and write the sentences your instructor says in Spanish.

1. The hotel is big.
2. The train is big.
3. The compact disc is little.
4. The park is big.
5. The hotel is not little.
6. The radio is not big.
7. The airplane is very big.
8. The restaurant is big.

2.5 ORAL EXERCISE

Complete the following sentences by choosing either **es** or **no es**, whichever fits.

1. El mosquito (es/no es) chiquito.
2. El tren (es/no es) chiquito.
3. El autobús (es/no es) chiquito.
4. El tractor (es/no es) grande.
5. El piano (es/no es) grande.
6. El radio (es/no es) chiquito.
7. El auto (es/no es) chiquito.
8. El hotel (es/no es) chiquito.
9. El disco compacto (es/no es) grande.
10. El sombrero (es/no es) grande.

2.6 ORAL EXERCISE

Your instructor will read a sentence in the affirmative. Repeat the same sentence in the negative by changing **es** to **no es**.

EXAMPLE: **El autobús es chiquito.**
ANSWER: **El autobús no es chiquito.**

1. El hotel es chiquito.
2. El mosquito es grande.
3. El auto es chiquito.
4. El disco compacto es grande.
5. El restaurante es chiquito.

6. El tren es chiquito.
7. El avión es chiquito.
8. El radio es grande.
9. El piano es chiquito.
10. El plato es grande.

 ## 2.7 GOING ON VACATION

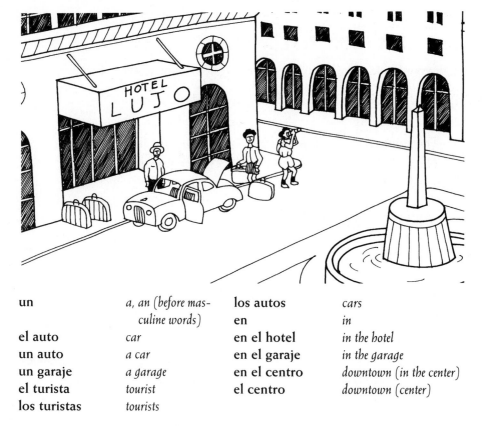

un	*a, an (before masculine words)*	**los autos**	*cars*
		en	*in*
el auto	*car*	**en el hotel**	*in the hotel*
un auto	*a car*	**en el garaje**	*in the garage*
un garaje	*a garage*	**en el centro**	*downtown (in the center)*
el turista	*tourist*	**el centro**	*downtown (center)*
los turistas	*tourists*		

2.8 ORAL EXERCISE

Answer the questions with the responses provided.

1. ¿Hay un hotel en el centro? Sí, hay un hotel en el centro.
2. ¿Hay turistas en el hotel? Sí, hay turistas en el hotel.
3. ¿Hay un garaje en el hotel? Sí, hay un garaje en el hotel.
4. ¿Hay autos en el garaje? Sí, hay autos en el garaje.
5. ¿Hay un restaurante en el hotel? Sí, hay un restaurante en el hotel.
6. ¿Hay turistas en el restaurante? Sí, hay turistas en el restaurante.
7. ¿ Hay rosbif en el restaurante? Sí, hay rosbif en el restaurante.
8. ¿ Hay bistec en el restaurante? Sí, hay bistec en el restaurante.
9. ¿ Hay sopa en el restaurante? Sí, hay sopa en el restaurante.
10. ¿ Hay café en el restaurante? Sí, hay café en el restaurante.

Can you do this exercise with your book closed?

Grammar: Definite and indefinite articles (masculine)

El (*The*) is a definite masculine article. **Un** (*A, an*) is an indefinite masculine article. **Los** (*The*) is a plural definite masculine article. **Unos** (*Some*) is a plural indefinite masculine article.

2.9 ORAL OR WRITTEN EXERCISE

For the following words, change the definite articles (**el** or **los**) to the indefinite articles (**un** or **unos**).

1. el garaje
2. los autobuses
3. el plato
4. el restaurante
5. los sombreros
6. el disco compacto
7. los radios
8. los aviones
9. el auto
10. el doctor
11. los parques
12. los favores

2.10 WORD BUILDER

> ### Pronunciation: Changing English words
> ### that end in -al into Spanish
>
> Most English words that end in -al are similar to Spanish words. These -al
> words are easy because you don't have to learn them; you already know them.
> Practice their Spanish pronunciation. Be sure to stress the last syllable of these
> words, like this: cen-TRAL.

List of **-al** words in Spanish (optional)

accidental	formal	oriental
el animal	gradual	original
beneficial	horizontal	personal
el canal	el hospital	plural
central	ideal	postal
el cereal	industrial	principal
colonial	instrumental	residencial
comercial	legal	rival
criminal	local	rural
cultural	manual	social
editorial	mental	total
elemental	el metal	tropical
experimental	moral	universal
federal	musical	vertical
festival	natural	
final	naval	

Note: The letter **m** is never doubled in Spanish. For example, the English
word *commercial* is spelled **comercial** in Spanish.

2.11 REVIEW—MINI-TEST

Close your book and write the words your instructor says in Spanish.

1. the canal
2. the cereal
3. the metal
4. the animal
5. the hospital
6. central
7. federal
8. tropical
9. colonial
10. local
11. final
12. formal
13. plural
14. natural

2.12 CONVERSATION VOCABULARY

la pera	*pear*	el sándwich	*sandwich*
la ensalada	*salad*	la carne	*meat*
el atún	*tuna fish*	el cine	*movie theater*
la sardina	*sardine*	enfrente de	*in front of*
de	*of*	¿Qué?	*What?*
la ensalada de salmón	*salmon salad*	y	*and*
la ensalada de atún	*tuna fish salad*	cerca del hotel	*close to, near the hotel (masc.)*
la ensalada de tomate	*tomato salad*	del	*of the (masc.)*
		su	*your, his, her*
		Es muy bonito.	*It's very pretty.*

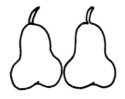

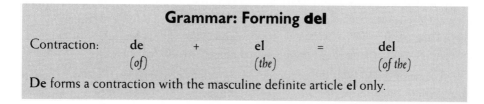

Grammar: Forming **del**

Contraction:	**de**	+	**el**	=	**del**
	(of)		*(the)*		*(of the)*

De forms a contraction with the masculine definite article **el** only.

2.13 ORAL OR WRITTEN EXERCISE

You will act out a restaurante scene at the end of this lesson. Before you do, practice the food vocabulary you have learned by giving the Spanish equivalent for each of the items listed.

EXAMPLE: **strawberry**
ANSWER: **la fresa**

1.	cheese	11.	salad
2.	roast beef	12.	tunafish
3.	beef steak	13.	cereal
4.	soup	14.	sardine
5.	coffee	15.	salad
6.	tea	16.	salmon salad
7.	chocolate	17.	tunafish salad
8.	grape	18.	tomato salad
9.	pear	19.	meat
10.	sandwich	20.	chili with meat

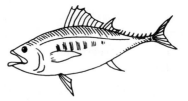

2.14 CONVERSATION

Señor and señora López and Mary and Robert have some questions about the menu at the restaurant where they are dining. Form groups of five students each. One student will play the waiter/waitress, the others will play the four customers. Each group will act out the restaurant scene for the class.

The following block will serve as a guide for your conversation. However, do not restrict yourself only to what is in the block.

<hr>

Ordering in a restaurant

(continued from Lesson 1)

SRA. LÓPEZ:	¿Hay bistec?
WAITER/WAITRESS:	Sí, señora. Hay bistec y rosbif.
SRA. LÓPEZ:	Bistec, por favor.
MARY:	¿Hay chocolate?
WAITER/WAITRESS:	Sí, señorita. Hay café, té y chocolate.
MARY:	Chocolate, por favor. Y un sándwich de rosbif.
ROBERT:	¿Hay sardinas?
WAITER/WAITRESS:	Sí, señor. Hay sardinas y salmón.
ROBERT:	Sardinas, por favor.
SR. LÓPEZ:	¿Hay ensalada?
WAITER/WAITRESS:	Sí, señor. Hay ensalada de tomate, ensalada de salmón y ensalada de atún.
SR. LÓPEZ:	Ensalada de atún, por favor.

<hr>

📼 2.15 CONVERSATION (OPTIONAL)

Form groups of two students each. Conduct a conversation between a tourist and a hotel clerk.

The following block will serve as a guide for your conversation. However, do not restrict yourself only to what is in the block.

<hr>

In the hotel

TOURIST:	¿Hay un garaje?
CLERK:	Sí, hay un garaje en el hotel.
TOURIST:	¿Hay un restaurante?
CLERK:	Sí, hay un restaurante en el hotel.
TOURIST:	¿Hay un cine?
CLERK:	Sí, hay un cine enfrente del hotel.
TOURIST:	¿Hay un parque cerca del hotel?
CLERK:	Sí, hay un parque cerca del hotel.

2.16 READING EXERCISE: LOS RESTAURANTES

In Lessons 1 and 2, you've learned how to order a meal in a restaurant. Now look at two ads for restaurants and see how much you can understand. Then complete the exercise that follows.

platos	*dishes*
sabrosos	*tasty*
más	*most*
ptas.	*pesetas (Spanish currency, now replaced by the euro)*

Read the following statements. If the statement refers to **el Faro Restaurante**, write **Faro**. If it refers to **Restaurante Vegetariano Artemisa**, write **Artemisa**. If it applies to both, write **Both**.

1. It serves Spanish food.
2. It is a vegetarian restaurant.
3. It serves Italian dishes.
4. It is the oldest Spanish restaurant in New York City.
5. Its ad lists the hours it is open.
6. Its ad lists a rating from a local newspaper.
7. Its ad lists a median price for a meal.
8. Its ad lists the address of the restaurant.
9. Its ad lists the telephone number of the restaurant.

2.17 WRITING EXERCISE

Look at the map below, which shows the city center of a small town in Mexico. Then write five sentences describing the city, using the words provided and following the example.

EXAMPLE: **Hay un parque. Es grande. No hay...**

Possible words: un parque, un hotel, un garaje, un cine, un restaurante, un autobús, hay, no hay, grande, chiquito, cerca de, enfrente de, bonito

VOCABULARY

NOUNS

el atún	*tuna fish*	la ensalada de salmón	*salmon salad*
el auto	*car*	la ensalada de tomate	*tomato salad*
el autobús	*bus*	el garaje	*garage*
la carne	*meat*	el hotel	*hotel*
el centro	*downtown (center)*	el parque	*park*
el cine	*movie theater*	la pera	*pear*
el elefante	*elephant*	el queso	*cheese*
la ensalada	*salad*	el restaurante	*restaurant*
la ensalada	*tuna fish salad*	el sándwich	*sandwich*
de atún		la sardina	*sardine*
		el turista	*tourist*

ADJECTIVES

chiquitito(a)   *very, very little; tiny*
popular   *popular (masc., fem.)*

OTHER WORDS AND EXPRESSIONS

cerca de   *close to, near*   **los**   *the (masc., pl.)*
de   *of*   **muy**   *very*
del   *of the (masc.)*   **no es**   *is not, isn't*
el   *the (masc., sing.)*   **¿Qué?**   *What?*
en   *in, on*   **su**   *your, his, her*
enfrente de   *in front of*   **un**   *a, an (masc., sing.)*
es muy bonito(a). *It's very pretty.* **unos**   *same (masc., pl.)*

OPTIONAL LIST

NOUNS

el animal   el festival
el canal   el hospital
el cereal   el metal

ADJECTIVES

accidental   mental
beneficial   moral
central   musical
colonial   natural
comercial   naval
criminal   oriental
cultural   original
editorial   personal
experimental   plural
federal   postal
final   principal
formal   residencial
gradual   rival
horizontal   rural
ideal   social
industrial   total
instrumental   tropical
legal   universal
local   vertical
manual

LESSON 3

✳

Con los amigos
- Feminine words
- **-ent** and **-ant** words in Spanish
- Definite and indefinite articles (feminine)
- The familiar form **tú**
- Greeting a friend

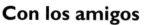 **3.1 HAVING LUNCH**

la	the (before feminine words)	deliciosa	delicious (fem.)
		la blusa	blouse
la rosa	rose	la casa	house
la fruta	fruit	una	a, an (before feminine words)
bonita	pretty (fem.)		
la señorita	young lady	blanca	white (fem.)

> **Grammar: Feminine words**
>
> In Spanish, most feminine words end in the letter **a.**

🎧 3.2 LISTENING EXERCISE

Repeat each sentence after your instructor says it, reading along in the book as you speak.

1. La rosa es bonita.
2. La blusa es bonita.
3. La blusa es blanca.
4. La casa es blanca.
5. La rosa es blanca.

6. La pera es una fruta.
7. La pera es deliciosa.
8. La fruta es deliciosa.
9. La rosa no es una fruta.
10. La ensalada es deliciosa.

3.3 ORAL EXERCISE

Answer the questions with the responses provided.

EXAMPLE: **¿Es bonita la blusa?** *Is the blouse pretty?*
ANSWER: **Sí, la blusa es bonita.** *Yes, the blouse is pretty.*

1. ¿Es bonita la rosa? Sí, la rosa es bonita.
2. ¿Es blanca la rosa? Sí, la rosa es blanca.
3. ¿Es blanca la casa? Sí, la casa es blanca.
4. ¿Es deliciosa la pera? Sí, la pera es deliciosa.
5. ¿Es deliciosa la fruta? Sí, la fruta es deliciosa.

6. ¿Es deliciosa la ensalada? Sí, la ensalada es deliciosa.

7. ¿Es deliciosa la sopa? Sí, la sopa es deliciosa.

8. ¿Es blanca la blusa? Sí, la blusa es blanca.

Can you do this exercise with your book closed?

3.4 WORD BUILDER

Pronunciation: Changing English words that end in **-ent** and **-ant** into Spanish

Most English words that end in -ent or -ant become Spanish words when you add the letter **e** to them. Stress the next to the last syllable of these words, like this: **pre-si-DEN-te**

List of **-ente** and **-ante** words in Spanish (optional)

abundante	el incidente
el accidente	el instante
el agente	interesante
el cliente	importante
competente	permanente
constante	presente
el continente	el presidente
conveniente	prominente
decente	prudente
diferente	significante
elegante	suficiente
evidente	tolerante
excelente	transparente
ignorante	

3.5 REVIEW—MINI-TEST

Close your book and write the words your instructor says in Spanish.
Remember to add -**e** to words that end in -**ent** or -**ant**.

1. the president
2. the accident
3. the continent
4. the client
5. the agent
6. the restaurant

7. the instant
8. important
9. present
10. competent
11. ignorant
12. elegant

Grammar: Definite and indefinite articles (feminine)

La (*The*) is a definite feminine article. **Una** (*A, an*) is an indefinite feminine article. **Las** (*The*) is a plural definite article. **Unas** (*Some*) is a plural indefinite article.

3.6 ORAL OR WRITTEN EXERCISE

For the words below, change the definite articles (**la** or **las**) to the indefinite articles (**una** or **unas**).

1. la rosa
2. las peras
3. las frutas
4. la ensalada

5. la blusa
6. las casas
7. la sardina
8. las señoritas

3.7 ORAL EXERCISE

The instructor will point to individual students to read the following sentences aloud.

1. El presidente es importante.
2. El presidente es competente.
3. El doctor es competente.
4. El restaurante es conveniente.

5. El restaurante es excelente.
6. El actor es excelente.
7. El cliente es importante.
8. El presidente no es ignorante.
9. El doctor no es ignorante.
10. África es un continente.

3.8 ORAL EXERCISE

Answer the questions with the responses provided.

EXAMPLE: **¿Hay suficiente café?** *Is there enough coffee?*
ANSWER: **Sí, hay suficiente café.** *Yes, there is enough coffee.*

1. ¿Hay suficiente chocolate? Sí, hay suficiente chocolate.
2. ¿Hay suficiente bistec? Sí, hay suficiente bistec.
3. ¿Hay suficiente rosbif? Sí, hay suficiente rosbif.
4. ¿Hay suficiente ensalada? Sí, hay suficiente ensalada.
5. ¿Hay suficiente sopa? Sí, hay suficiente sopa.
6. ¿Hay suficiente cereal? Sí, hay suficiente cereal.
7. ¿Hay suficiente queso? Sí, hay suficiente queso.

Can you do this exercise with your book closed?

3.9 REVIEW–MINI-TEST (COGNATES)

Close your book and write in Spanish the English words your instructor says.

1. piano	13. favor	25. tropical
2. radio	14. vigor	26. error
3. tractor	15. auto	27. tumor
4. hotel	16. diploma	28. formal
5. mosquito	17. central	29. final
6. actor	18. hospital	30. colonial
7. doctor	19. director	31. mental
8. motor	20. humor	32. plural
9. color	21. federal	33. natural
10. animal	22. local	34. total
11. canal	23. honor	35. chocolate
12. cereal	24. metal	36. excellent

Grammar: The familiar form **tú**

In Spanish we have two words for *you*: **usted** and **tú**. **Tú** is the familiar form. The very word "familiar" gives you a clue to its use. You use **tú**, the familiar *you*, when you are speaking to members of your family. You also use **tú** when speaking to close friends. In some countries, such as Spain, the familiar **tú** is used with almost everyone. You have already learned one use of **tú**: ¿**Cómo estás?** is the familiar way to ask how someone is.

3.10 CONVERSATION VOCABULARY

usted	*you (formal)*
tú	*you (fam.)*
y	*and*
¿Y usted?	*And you? (formal)*
¿Y tú?	*And you? (fam.)*
¿Cómo se llama usted?	*What is your name? (formal)*
Me llamo…	*My name is…*

Review the vocabulary on page 6 before going on to the conversation that follows.

3.11 CONVERSATION

Practice greeting a friend in groups of two students each.

Sample conversation

FIRST STUDENT: Buenas noches, *(name)*. *Good evening, (name).*
SECOND STUDENT: Buenas noches. *Good evening.*
FIRST STUDENT: ¿Cómo estás? *How are you? (fam.)*
SECOND STUDENT: Bien, gracias. ¿Y tú? *Fine, thank you. And you? (fam.)*
FIRST STUDENT: Bien, gracias. *Fine, thank you.*

The following block will serve as a guide for your conversation. However, do not restrict yourself only to what is in the block.

Greeting a friend

FIRST STUDENT: Buenos días, (name).
SECOND STUDENT: Buenos días.
FIRST STUDENT: ¿Cómo estás?
SECOND STUDENT: Bien, gracias. ¿Y tú?
FIRST STUDENT: Bien, gracias.

FIRST STUDENT: Buenas tardes, (name).
SECOND STUDENT: Buenas tardes.
FIRST STUDENT: ¿Cómo está usted?
SECOND STUDENT: Bien, gracias. ¿Y usted?
FIRST STUDENT: Bien, gracias.

3.12 READING EXERCISE: POR LA NOCHE

Look at the following list of activities available one evening in Madrid, Spain. Then answer the questions that follow.

GUÍA DE ACTIVIDADES

CINE

"40 días y 40 noches"
Cine Tívoli
c/ Alcalá, 80 Tel.: 915782773
13:00, 15:30, 18:00, 20:30

"La casa de mi vida"
Cine Luna
c/ Luna, 2 Tel.: 915224752
14:30, 16:30, 18:30, 20:30

TEATRO

14 de junio, 17:00
Festival de Shakespeare
Círculo de Bellas Artes

"La Bella y la Bestia"
Samarkanda Teatro
16 de junio, 20:00

MÚSICA

El Festival Flamenco "La Yerbabuena"
Plaza de Atocha
14 de junio, 14:00

El grupo del folk L'Arca
Café Teatro Pícolo
12 de junio, 22:30

RESTAURANTES

Casa Lucio, c/ Cava Baja, 35 Tel.:
913653252
Precio: Todos los precios

Las Cuatro Estaciones
c/ General Ibáñez Ibero, 5 Tel.:
915536305 · Salones privados.
Precio: Todos los precios

---

1. Today is June 14th. What two options do you have for music and theater?
2. On what day can you see a folk group?
3. On what day can you see "La Bella y la Bestia" at the Samarkanda Theater?
4. Where is the Festival Flamenco and what day?
5. What movie is playing at the Tívoli?
6. Where is the movie "La casa de mi vida" playing?
7. Which restaurant has private dining rooms?

3.13 WRITING EXERCISE

Write five sentences saying what is going on in the places indicated. Follow the example.

EXAMPLE: **Cine Tívoli**
ANSWER: **En el Cine Tívoli exhiben "40 días y 40 noches."**

1. Cine Luna
2. Plaza de Atocha
3. Samarkanda Teatro
4. Café Teatro Pícolo
5. Círculo de Bellas Artes

VOCABULARY

NOUNS

		ADJECTIVES	
la rosa	*rose*	**blanco(a)**	*white*
la blusa	*blouse*	**bonito(a)**	*pretty*
la casa	*house*	**delicioso(a)**	*delicious*
la fruta	*fruit*		
la señorita	*young lady*		

OTHER WORDS AND EXPRESSIONS

la	*the (fem., sing)*
las	*the (fem., pl.)*
tú	*you (fam.)*
una	*a, an (before feminine words)*
unas	*some (fem., pl.)*
usted	*you (formal)*

OPTIONAL LIST

NOUNS

el accidente
el agente
el cliente
el continente
el incidente
el instante
el presidente

ADJECTIVES

abundante
competente
constante
conveniente
decente
diferente
elegante
evidente
excelente
ignorante
importante

instante
interesante
permanente
presente
prominente
prudente
significante
suficiente
tolerante
transparente

LESSON 4

La vida en la ciudad

- Gender of nouns
- Colors
- **-ic** words in Spanish
- Noun and adjective agreement (number and gender)
- Nationalities
- Asking for country of origin

Grammar: Masculine and feminine words

In Spanish, most words that end in the letter **o** are masculine. Most words that end in the letter **a** are feminine. For more information about the plural forms, see page 39.

4.1 ORAL EXERCISE

Repeat the following masculine and feminine words after the instructor says them.

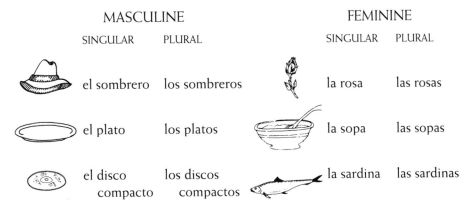

MASCULINE		FEMININE	
SINGULAR	PLURAL	SINGULAR	PLURAL
el sombrero	los sombreros	la rosa	las rosas
el plato	los platos	la sopa	las sopas
el disco compacto	los discos compactos	la sardina	las sardinas

4.2 DRAWING WITH COLORS

rojo(a)	*red*
verde	*green (masc., fem.)*
blanco(a)	*white*
azul	*blue (masc., fem.)*
gris	*gray (masc., fem.)*
rosado(a)	*pink*
negro(a)	*black*
amarillo(a)	*yellow*
color café, marrón	*brown (masc., fem.)*
morado(a)	*purple*
anaranjado(a)	*orange*
el canario	*canary*
la gasolina	*gasoline*
la pluma	*pen, feather*
¡Ay no!	*Oh no!*
la aspirina	*aspirin*

Review the following adjectives in their masculine and feminine forms.

MASCULINE	FEMININE	
bonito	bonita	*pretty*
blanco	blanca	*white*
negro	negra	*black*
chiquito	chiquita	*little*
delicioso	deliciosa	*delicious*
amarillo	amarilla	*yellow*

Grammar: Nouns and adjectives together

Use masculine adjectives with masculine nouns.

EXAMPLE: **El sombrero es bonito.**

Use feminine adjectives with feminine nouns.

EXAMPLE: **La blusa es bonita.**

4.3 ORAL EXERCISE

Choose the correct adjective in each sentence. Remember to use adjectives that end in -o with nouns that end in -o. Use adjectives that end in -a with nouns that end in -a.

1. El plato es (blanco/blanca).
2. El auto es (negro/negra).
3. La casa es (blanco/blanca).
4. La pluma es (chiquito/chiquita).
5. El canario es (chiquito/chiquita).
6. El sombrero es (bonito/bonita).
7. La blusa es (bonito/bonita).
8. La sopa es (delicioso/deliciosa).
9. La rosa es (bonito/bonita).
10. La ensalada es (delicioso/deliciosa).
11. La fruta es (delicioso/deliciosa).
12. La sardina es (chiquito/chiquita).
13. El canario es (amarillo/amarilla).
14. La blusa es (amarillo/amarilla).

4.4 ORAL EXERCISE

Answer the following questions.

EXAMPLE: **¿Es chiquita la pluma?**
ANSWER: **Sí, la pluma es chiquita.**
EXAMPLE: **¿Es chiquita la casa?**
ANSWER: **No, la casa no es chiquita.**

1. ¿Es rojo el sombrero? Sí,...
2. ¿Es rosada la blusa? Sí,...
3. ¿Es verde la pluma? Sí,...
4. ¿Es chiquita la casa? No,...
5. ¿Es roja la aspirina? No,...
6. ¿Es azul el canario? No,...
7. ¿Es blanco el auto? Sí,...
8. ¿Es negra la rosa? No,...

4.5 ORAL OR WRITTEN EXERCISE

Give the feminine form of the following adjectives.

1. blanco   4. chiquito
2. negro   5. delicioso
3. bonito   6. amarillo

4.6 WORD BUILDER

Pronunciation: Changing English words that end in **-ic** into Spanish

Most English words that end in -ic become Spanish words when you add the letter -o to them. These words carry the stress on the letter which has the written accent.

List of **-ico** words in Spanish (optional)

Atlántico	diplomático	eléctrico	el público
atómico	dramático	fantástico	romántico
democrático	el elástico	Pacífico	el tónico

4.7 REVIEW—MINI-TEST

Your instructor will read the previous list of Spanish words to you in English. Close your book and write them in Spanish. After you have finished the test, open your book and check your list against the list in the book. Don't forget to add **o** and an accent to the Spanish words.

Grammar: Noun and adjective agreement (number and gender)

	SINGULAR	PLURAL
MASCULINE	el rancho bonito	los ranchos bonitos
FEMININE	la casa bonita	las casas bonitas
MASCULINE	el sombrero chiquito	los sombreros chiquitos
FEMININE	la blusa chiquita	las blusas chiquitas
MASCULINE	el auto blanco	los autos blancos
FEMININE	la rosa blanca	las rosas blancas
MASCULINE	el plato delicioso	los platos deliciosos
FEMININE	la sopa deliciosa	las sopas deliciosas
MASCULINE	el hotel fantástico	los hoteles fantásticos
FEMININE	la ensalada fantástica	las ensaladas fantásticas
MASCULINE	el tractor amarillo	los tractores amarillos
FEMININE	la pera amarilla	las peras amarillas

To form the plural in Spanish, add the letters to nouns and adjectives that end in a vowel. Adjectives should agree with nouns in gender (masculine or feminine) and number (singular or plural). To form the plural of Spanish nouns and adjectives ending in a consonant, add -**es**.

There are some masculine nouns which don't end in -**o** and some feminine nouns which don't end in -**a**.

   EXAMPLES: **el hotel, el tractor, la complexión**

However, when such nouns are used with adjectives, the adjective still changes to show the noun's gender.

   EXAMPLES: **el hotel fantástico, la complexión bonita**

4.8 LIVING IN A CITY

los	*the (masc. pl.)*	la violeta	*violet*
las	*the (fem. pl.)*	las violetas	*violets*
unos	*some (masc. pl.)*	la motocicleta	*motorcycle*
unas	*some (fem. pl.)*	son	*are*
el edificio moderno(a)	*building modern*	**las mariposas**	*butterflies*
El edificio es moderno.	*The building is modern.*	**el chocolate**	*chocolate drink*
la mariposa	*butterfly*	**los chocolates**	*chocolates (candy)*

4.9 LISTENING EXERCISE

Repeat each sentence after your instructor says it, reading along in the book as you speak.

1. La rosa es bonita.
2. Las rosas son bonitas.
3. La casa es blanca.
4. Las casas son blancas.
5. El sombrero es bonito.
6. Los sombreros son bonitos.
7. Las peras son deliciosas.
8. La violeta es chiquita.
9. Las violetas son chiquitas.
10. El chocolate es delicioso.
11. Los chocolates son deliciosos.
12. La mariposa es bonita.
13. Las mariposas son bonitas.
14. Las fresas son deliciosas.
15. La motocicleta es fantástica.
16. El edificio es moderno.

4.10 ORAL EXERCISE

As your instructor points to individual students each should give the plural of the word indicated.

EXAMPLE: **el sombrero**
ANSWER: **los sombreros**

1. el disco compacto	7. bonito	13. delicioso
2. la pluma	8. blanco	14. deliciosa
3. la pera	9. bonita	15. chiquito
4. el mosquito	10. blanca	16. chiquita
5. la mariposa	11. negro	17. fantástico
6. la violeta	12. negra	18. el edificio

4.11 CONVERSATION VOCABULARY

italiano	*Italian (masc.)*	**Soy...**	*I am...*
italiana	*Italian (fem.)*	**No soy...**	*I am not...*
americano	*American (masc.)*	**Somos...**	*We are...*
americana	*American (fem.)*	**No somos...**	*We are not...*
colombiano	*Colombian (masc.)*	**¿Es usted...?**	*Are you...?*
colombiana	*Colombian (fem.)*	**¿Eres...?**	*Are you...? (fam.)*
puertorriqueño	*Puerto Rican (masc.)*	**Son americanos.**	*They are Americans. (masc.)*
puertorriqueña	*Puerto Rican (fem.)*	**Son americanas.**	*They are Americans. (fem.)*

In Spanish, you do not say *I am an American*. You simply say **Soy americano.**

SOME OTHER HISPANIC NATIONALITIES (OPTIONAL)

argentino(a)	*Argentine*	**dominicano(a)**	*Dominican*
boliviano(a)	*Bolivian*	**mexicano(a)**	*Mexican*
cubano(a)	*Cuban*	**panameño(a)**	*Panamanian*
chileno(a)	*Chilean*	**venezolano(a)**	*Venezuelan*

Spelling

Notice that in Spanish you don't use a capital letter for nationalities.

> EXAMPLES: **¿Es usted americano?** *Are you an American?*
>
> (when you ask a man or a boy)
>
> **¿Es usted americana?** *Are you an American?*
>
> (when you ask a woman or a girl)

4.12 CONVERSATION

Form groups of two students and conduct a conversation about nationalities. Ask your partner as many questions about nationalities as you can. He or she will answer them.

The following block will serve as a guide for your conversation. However, do not restrict yourself only to what is in the block.

Talking about nationalities

FIRST STUDENT: ¿Es Frank americano?
SECOND STUDENT: Sí, Frank es americano.

FIRST STUDENT: ¿Es Gino italiano?
SECOND STUDENT: Sí, Gino es italiano.

FIRST STUDENT: ¿Es Susan americana?
SECOND STUDENT: Sí, Susan es americana.

FIRST STUDENT: ¿Es usted americano? (Second student is male.)
SECOND STUDENT: Sí, soy americano.

FIRST STUDENT: ¿Es usted americana? (Second student is female.)
SECOND STUDENT: Sí, soy americana.

FIRST STUDENT: ¿Eres mexicana? (Second student is a close female friend.)
SECOND STUDENT: No, no soy mexicana.

FIRST STUDENT: ¿Eres italiana? (Second student is a close female friend.)
SECOND STUDENT: No, no soy italiana.

FIRST STUDENT: ¿Eres americano? (Second student is a close male friend.)
SECOND STUDENT: Sí, soy americano.

FIRST STUDENT:	¿Eres americana? (Second student is a close female friend.)	
SECOND STUDENT:	Sí, soy americana.	
FIRST STUDENT:	¿Eres italiano? (Second student is a close male friend.)	
SECOND STUDENT:	No, no soy italiano.	

Grammar: Masculine and feminine adjectives

Remember: If you are a man or a boy, use a masculine adjective.

EXAMPLE: **Soy americano.** *I am (an) American.*

If you are a woman or a girl, use a feminine adjective.

EXAMPLE: **Soy americana.** *I am (an) American.*

If your refer to a man or a boy, use a masculine adjective.

EXAMPLE: **Gino es italiano.** *Gino is (an) Italian.*

If you refer to a woman or a girl, use a feminine adjective.

EXAMPLE: **María es italiana.** *María is (an) Italian.*

If you refer to two or more men, or to a mixed group, use a masculine plural adjective.

EXAMPLES: **Gino y María son italianos.** *Gino and María are Italian(s).*
Gino y Marcos son italianos. *Gino and Marcos are Italian(s).*

If you refer to two or more women, use a feminine plural adjective.

EXAMPLE: **María y Carola son italianas.** *María and Carola are Italian(s).*

4.13 OPTIONAL VOCABULARY

la gardenia	*gardenia*
las gardenias	*gardenias*
fresco(a)	*fresh*
el tulipán	*tulip*
los tulipanes	*tulips*
la montaña	*mountain*
Holanda	*Holland*
en Holanda	*in Holland*
en Costa Rica	*in Costa Rica*
en el Canadá	*in Canada*
en el Ecuador	*in Ecuador*
el pino	*pine tree*
los pinos	*pine trees*
el geranio	*geranium*

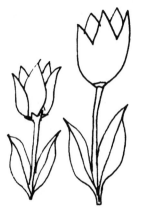

los geranios	geraniums	los geranios rojos	red geraniums
la begonia	begonia		
las rosas blancas	white roses	las begonias blancas	white begonias
las rosas rojas	red roses		
las gardenias blancas	white gardenias	las begonias amarillas	yellow begonias
los tulipanes blancos	white tulips	la fruta fresca	fresh fruit
		las frutas deliciosas	delicious fruits
los tulipanes rojos	red tulips		
		las montañas inmensas	immense mountains
los tulipanes amarillos	yellow tulips	los pinos inmensos	immense pine trees
los tulipanes fantásticos	fantastic tulips	los canarios amarillos	yellow canaries

Note: In Spanish, we say **el Canadá** instead of **Canada**, and **el Ecuador** instead of **Ecuador**.

4.14 ORAL EXERCISE

Answer the questions with the responses provided.

1. ¿Hay tulipanes blancos? Sí, hay tulipanes blancos.
2. ¿Hay tulipanes rojos? Sí, hay tulipanes rojos.
3. ¿Hay tulipanes amarillos? Sí, hay tulipanes amarillos.
4. ¿Hay tulipanes fantásticos en Holanda? Sí, hay tulipanes fantásticos en Holanda.
5. ¿Hay rosas rojas en el Ecuador? Sí, hay rosas rojas en el Ecuador.
6. ¿Hay rosas blancas? Sí, hay rosas blancas.
7. ¿Hay rosas amarillas? Sí, hay rosas amarillas.
8. ¿Hay gardenias blancas en Puerto Rico? Sí, hay gardenias blancas en Puerto Rico.
9. ¿Hay begonias blancas? Sí, hay begonias blancas.
10. ¿Hay canarios amarillos? Sí, hay canarios amarillos.
11. ¿Hay frutas deliciosas en Costa Rica? Sí, hay frutas deliciosas en Costa Rica.
12. ¿Hay fruta fresca en el restaurante? Sí, hay fruta fresca en el restaurante.
13. ¿Hay pinos inmensos en el Canadá? Sí, hay pinos inmensos en el Canadá.
14. ¿Hay montañas inmensas en México? Sí, hay montañas inmensas en México.

Can you do this exercise with your book closed?

Pronunciation

Pronounce **montañas inmensas** with big, round a's. Pronounce these words like this: **mon-TA-ñas in-MEN-sas**.

4.15 READING EXERCISE: LOS RESTAURANTES ÉTNICOS

In Lesson 4 you've learned a variety of nationalities. Many nationalities are cognates. See how many of the following ethnic restaurants' nationalities you can figure out. Then do the exercise that follows.

■ **ÁRABES**

AL-MOUNIA. Recoletos, 5 (Centro). Tel. 453 08 28
BAALBACK. Orense, 70 (Tetuán). Tel. 572 07 86

■ **ARGENTINOS**

EL LOCRO. Trujillos, 2 (Centro). Tel. 522 43 82
LA OMA. Rafael Herrera, 11. Tel. 315 09 08
LA PAMPA. Amparo, 61 (lavapiés). Tel. 228 04 49
LA PAMPA II. La Bola, 8 (Centro). Tel. 542 44 12
LA QUERENCIA. Lope de Vega, 16. Tel. 429 41 83

■ **BRASILEÑOS**

ZARA. Infantes, 5 (Centro). Tel. 532 20 74

■ **CHILENOS**

EL RINCÓN CHILENO. García Luna, 4 (Prosperidad). Tel. 416 99 66

■ **CHINOS**

CHI-ZHI-JU. Capitán Haya, 55 (edificio posterior). Tel. 279 91 31

■ **COREANOS**

SEÚL. Avda. de Nazaret, 10 (Colonia del Retiro). Tel. 409 70 83
SHILA. Panamá, 4 (plaza de Cuzco). Tel. 457 88 33

■ **ESCANDINAVOS**

BELLMAN. Marqués de Casa Riera, 4. Tel. 531 69 00

■ **FRANCESES**

LA FOLIE. Hermosilla, 7 (Salamanca). Tel. 431 10 72
LE BISTROQUET. Conde, 4 (Centro). Tel. 247 10 75
LA MARMITE. Plaza de San Amaro, 8. Tel. 279 92 61

■ **FILIPINOS**

SULÚ. Paseo de la Castellana, 172 (Chamartín). Tel 259 64 54

■ **GRIEGOS**

TABERNA GRIEGA. Tesoro, 6. Tel. 532 18 92.
LA BROCHETTERIE. San Vicente Ferrer, 33 (Noviciado). Tel. 532 14 75

■ **INDIOS**

ADRISCH. Plaza Conde de Toreno, 2 (plaza de España). Tels. 542 94 98 y 542 93 74

■ **NORTEAMERICANOS**

ARMSTRONGS. Jovellanos, 5 (frente teatro Zarzuela). Tel. 522 42 30
FOSTER HOLLYWOOD. Magallanes, 1 (Chamberí). Tel. 448 91 65. Apolonio Morales, 3 (Chamartín). Tel. 457 79 11, Tamayo y Baus, 1 (Centro). Tel. 531 51 15. Calle del Cristo (Majadahonda). Tel. 638 67 91. Avenida de Brasil, 14-16 (Teután). Tel. 455 16 88. Velázquez, 80 (Salamanca). Tel. 435 61 28. Guzmán el Bueno, 100 (Chamberí). Tel 234 49 23

Match the restaurant on the left with its nationality on the right.

1.	La Marmite	a.	Philippine
2.	Chi-Zhi-Ju	b.	Greek
3.	La Querencia	c.	Arabic
4.	Adrisch	d.	French
5.	Shila	e.	Chilean
6.	Bellman	f.	Argentine
7.	El Rincón Chileno	g.	North American
8.	Baalbeck	h.	Brazilian
9.	Sulú	i.	Indian
10.	Taberna Griega	j.	Chinese
11.	Armstrongs	k.	Korean
12.	Zara	l.	Scandinavian

4.16 WRITING EXERCISE

Use the information from the list of restaurants on page 44 and write six sentences using the nationalities provided and following the example.

EXAMPLE: **brasileño**
ANSWER: **Zara es un restaurante brasileño.**

Nacionalidades: argentino, chileno, chino, filipino, indio, norteamericano

VOCABULARY

NOUNS

la aspirina	*aspirin*
el canario	*canary*
los chocolates	*chocolates (candy)*
el edificio	*building*
la gasolina	*gasoline*
la mariposa	*butterfly*
la motocicleta	*motorcycle*
la pluma	*pen, feather*
la violeta	*violet*

ADJECTIVES

amarillo(a)	*yellow*	italiano(a)	*Italian*
americano(a)	*American*	moderno(a)	*modern*
anaranjado(a)	*orange*	morado(a)	*purple*
azul	*blue (masc., fem.)*	negro(a)	*black*
blanco(a)	*white*	puertorriqueño(a)	*Puerto Rican*
colombiano(a)	*Colombian*	rojo(a)	*red*
color café, marrón	*brown (masc., fem.)*	rosado(a)	*pink*
gris	*gray (masc., fem.)*	verde	*green (masc., fem.)*

OTHER WORDS AND EXPRESSIONS

¡Ay no!	*Oh no!*
¿Eres…?	*Are you…? (fam.)*
¿Es usted…?	*Are you…?*
No somos…	*We are not…*
No son…	*They are not…*
No soy…	*I am not…*
Somos…	*We are…*
Son…	*They are…*
Soy…	*I am…*

OPTIONAL LIST

NOUNS

la begonia	el geranio
el Canadá	Holanda
Costa Rica	la montaña
el Ecuador	el pino
el elástico	el público
la gardenia	el tónico
	el tulipán

ADJECTIVES

argentino(a)	dramático(a)
Atlántico(a)	eléctrico(a)
atómico(a)	fantástico(a)
boliviano(a)	fresco(a)
cubano(a)	mexicano(a)
chileno(a)	Pacífico(a)
democrático(a)	panameño(a)
diplomático(a)	romántico(a)
dominicano(a)	venezolano(a)

LESSON 5

❋

En el centro

- The present tense of **-ar** verbs, singular forms
- Forming questions
- Changing **-ous** words into Spanish

Grammar: Singular forms of regular **-ar** verbs in the present tense

Spanish verbs whose infinitives end in **-ar** are conjugated the same way.

EXAMPLE, SPANISH -AR VERBS:

progresar	*to progress*	**comprar**	*to buy*
estudiar	*to study*	**hablar**	*to speak*

Here are the **tú** forms of these **-ar** verbs.

EXAMPLES: **tú progresas, tú estudias, tú compras, tú hablas**

Usted forms* for regular **-ar** forms in the present tense are the same as the **tú** forms, but without the final **-s**. Here are the **usted** forms of the same **-ar** verbs.

EXAMPLES: **usted progresa, usted estudia, usted compra, usted habla**

*As you will learn in the next lesson, the **usted** form can also be used with third person subjects, such as *he, she, Susan, Robert,* etc.

Here are all three singular forms. Notice that the **yo** form ends in **-o**.

Compro...	*I buy...*	**Estudio.**	*I study.*
¿Compra usted...?	*Do you buy...?*	**¿Estudia usted?**	*Do you study?*
¿Compras tú...?	*Do you buy...? (fam.)*	**¿Estudias tú?**	*Do you study? (fam.)*
Hablo...	*I speak (I talk)...*	**Progreso.**	*I progress.*
¿Habla usted...?	*Do you speak...?*	**¿Progresa usted?**	*Do you progress?*
¿Hablas tú...?	*Do you speak...? (fam.)*	**¿Progresas tú?**	*Do you progress? (fam.)*

Note: Subject pronouns such as **yo** and **tú** are frequently dropped with a conjugated verb. Stress the next to the last syllable of verbs in the present tense. Repeat the following Spanish words after your instructor says them.

Yo progreso.	*I progress.*	**Tú estudias.**	*You study. (fam.)*
Yo hablo…	*I speak, (talk)…*	**Usted compra…**	*You buy…*

Remember to stress the next to the last syllable firmly, like this: **pro-GRE-so, es-TU-dias, COM-pra, HA-blo.**

5.1 BUYING FOOD

el mercado	*market*	el melón	*cantaloupe*
el supermercado	*supermarket*	el español	*Spanish*
la tienda	*store*	el inglés	*English*
la clase	*class*	un poco	*a little bit*
en casa	*at home*	la estación de gasolina	*gasoline station*
en la clase	*in class*		
los pantalones	*trousers, pants*	los calcetines	*socks*
		la flor	*flower*
los guantes	*gloves*		

Grammar: Forming questions

To change a sentence into a question, reverse the order of the words so the verb comes before the subject.

EXAMPLES:

¿Progresa usted?	*Do you progress?*
¿Estudia usted?	*Do you study?*
¿Compra usted…?	*Do you buy…?*
¿Habla usted…?	*Do you speak…? (fam.)*
¿Progresas tú?	*Do you progress? (fam.)*

5.2 LISTENING EXERCISE

Repeat each sentence after your instructor says it, reading along in the book as you speak.

1. ¿Habla usted inglés?
2. Hablo inglés.
3. Hablo español.
4. Hablo español en la clase.
5. Hablo inglés en casa.
6. Estudio español.
7. Estudio español en la clase.
8. Compro peras en el mercado.
9. Compro gasolina en la estación de gasolina.

10. Compro blusas en la tienda.

11. Compro pantalones en la tienda.

12. Compro guantes en la tienda.

5.3 ORAL EXERCISE

Answer the questions with the responses provided.

1. ¿Compra usted peras en el mercado? Sí, compro peras en el mercado.

2. ¿Compra usted melones en el mercado? Sí, compro melones en el mercado.

3. ¿Compra usted flores en el mercado? Sí, compro flores en el mercado.

4. ¿Compra usted gasolina en la estación de gasolina? Sí, compro gasolina en la estación de gasolina.

5. ¿Compra usted blusas en la tienda? Sí, compro blusas en la tienda.

6. ¿Habla usted español? Sí, hablo español—un poco.

7. ¿Habla usted español en la clase? Sí, hablo español en la clase.

8. ¿Habla usted inglés? Sí, hablo inglés.

9. ¿Habla usted inglés en casa? Sí, hablo inglés en casa.

10. ¿Progresa usted en la clase? Sí, progreso mucho en la clase.

11. ¿Estudia usted español? Sí, estudio español.

5.4 WORD BUILDER

Pronunciation: Changing English words that end in -ous into Spanish

Most English words that end in -ous become Spanish words when you change the -ous to -oso.

Stress the next to the last syllable of these words, like this: fa-MO-so.

List of -oso words in Spanish (optional)

delicioso	precioso
curioso	religioso
famoso	victorioso
furioso	fabuloso
generoso	misterioso

5.5 REVIEW–MINI-TEST

Close your book and write in Spanish the words your instructor says in English. Remember to change the final -ous in English to -oso.

1. famous
2. furious
3. delicious
4. curious
5. generous

6. precious
7. victorious
8. religious
9. fabulous

5.6 LISTENING VOCABULARY

la ciudad	*city*	**el museo**	*museum*
el teatro	*theater*	**extraordinario(a)**	*extraordinary*
excelente	*excellent (masc., fem.)*	**la pintura**	*painting*
Hay mucho tráfico.	*There is a lot of traffic.*	**la estatua**	*statue*
el camión	*truck*	**muchas flores tropicales**	*many tropical flowers*
el parque lindo	*beautiful park*	**siempre hay**	*there is always, there are always*

⊡ 5.7 LISTENING EXERCISE

Listen to the following composition as your instructor reads it aloud. Read along in your book, paying particular attention to the pronunciation of the Spanish words.

Caracas, Venezuela

Caracas es una ciudad muy interesante. En Caracas hay muchos edificios modernos. Hay hoteles, teatros y restaurantes excelentes. Los museos de Caracas son extraordinarios. En los museos hay pinturas y estatuas excelentes.

Caracas es una ciudad grande. Hay mucho tráfico. Hay autos, camiones, autobuses y motocicletas. Hay parques lindos en Caracas. En los parques hay estatuas muy bonitas y muchas flores tropicales. En los parques siempre hay muchos turistas americanos.

5.8 ORAL EXERCISE (OPTIONAL)

Your instructor will point to individual students who will read one sentence in the composition above and translate it into English.

5.9 READING EXERCISE

Now read aloud a whole paragraph of the composition. Try to read as smoothly as you can.

5.10 READING EXERCISE: LOS MUSEOS

In this lesson, you learned the word for museum. There are many different kinds of museums and many of the words you use to talk about museums and their contents are cognates. Look at the following list of museums in Madrid. Then answer the questions that follow.

MUSEOS

ARQUEOLÓGICO. Consultar sección Planes con Niños.

LÁZARO GALDIANO. Serrano. 122. Teléfono 26160 84. Pintura europea, artes decorativas, antigüedades egipcias, griegas y romanas.

REAL JARDÍN BOTÁNICO. Plaza de Murillo, 2 (metro Atocha). Tel. 420 35 68. Horario, de 10 a 19 h. Precio: 75 PUS, adultos; 50 ptas, estudiantes con carné; grupos acompañados de profesor, 25 ptas.; mayores de 65 años, gratis. Siglo XVIII Dos secciones: herbario y cultivo. Contiene ejemplares raros de la flora nacional y especies exóticas.

ESPAÑOL DE ARTE CONTEMPORÁNEO. Avenida de Juan de Herrera, 2 (Ciudad Universitaria). Tel. 449 7150. Horario: 10 a 18 h., domingos de 10 a 14 horas. Lunes cerrado. Entrada gratuita para españoles con DNI. Especialidad: artes plásticas contemporáneas y fotografía.

MUNICIPAL Fuencarral, 78. Tels 52166 56 y 522 57 32. Horario: de 10 a 14 y de 17 a 21 h.; domingos, de 10 a 14 h. Cerrado, lunes y festivos. Entrada gratuita. Historia de Madrid de los siglos XVI a XX y exposición permanente desde la Prehistoria a 1875. Modelo de Madrid de 1830.

ROMÁNTICO. San Mateo, 13. Tels. 44 10 45 y 448 10 71. Horario: de martes a sábado, de 10 a 15 h.; domingos, de 10 a 14 h Precio: 200 ptas. Entrada gratuita con DNI Cerrado, lunes. Colecciones de pintura, muebles y ajuar del periodo romántico (1820-1868).

el jardín	*the garden*
el niño	*the child*
sobre	*about*

Now complete the descriptions of what you may see in each museum. Choose from the list of words provided and answer based on the information contained in the listing. Answer in complete Spanish sentences, following the model.

LIST OF ANSWERS:

flores
fotografía
pintura del período romántico
artefactos arqueológicos para niños
pintura europea
información sobre la historia de Madrid

EXAMPLE: **el Museo Arqueológico**
ANSWER: **En el Museo Arqueológico hay artefactos arqueológicos para niños.**

1. el Museo Romántico
2. el Museo Español de Arte Contemporáneo
3. el Museo Lázaro Galdiano
4. el Real Jardín Botánico
5. el Museo Municipal

5.11 WRITING EXERCISE

Use the museum listings on page 55 to write sentences following the examples. Write four full sentences, each one about a different museum. Be sure to look at the museum listings to find words and phrases you can use in your sentences.

EXAMPLES: **El Museo Arqueológico es interesante.**
             En el Real Jardín hay dos secciones.

1. El Museo Lázaro Galdiano
2. El Real Jardín Botánico
3. El Museo Español de Arte Contemporáneo
4. El Museo Romántico

VOCABULARY

NOUNS

los calcetines	*socks*	el mercado	*market*
el camión	*truck*	el melón	*cantaloupe*
la clase	*class*	el museo	*museum*
la ciudad	*city*	los pantalones	*trousers, pants*
el español	*Spanish*	el parque	*park*
la estación de gasolina	*gas station*	la pintura	*painting*
		el supermercado	*supermarket*
la estatua	*statue*	el teatro	*theater*
la flor	*flower*	la tienda	*store*
los guantes	*gloves*	el tráfico	*traffic*
el inglés	*English*		

VERBS

comprar	*to buy*	hablar	*to speak, to talk*
estudiar	*to study*	progresar	*to progress*

ADJECTIVES

excelente	*excellent (masc., fem.)*	lindo(a)	*beautiful*
extraordinario(a)	*extraordinary*	tropical	*tropical (masc., fem.)*

OTHER WORDS AND EXPRESSIONS

en casa	*at home*	siempre hay	*there is always, there are always*
en la clase	*in class*		
Hay mucho tráfico.	*There is a lot of traffic.*	un poco	*a little bit*

OPTIONAL LIST

ADJECTIVES

curioso(a)	generoso(a)
delicioso(a)	misterioso(a)
fabuloso(a)	precioso(a)
famoso(a)	religioso(a)
furioso(a)	victorioso(a)

LESSON 6

✳

El trabajo
- Negating sentences
- **-ble** words in Spanish
- How to use the singular present tense of **-ar** verbs
- Questions with **dónde**
- Talking about where people work

Grammar: Negating sentences

To make a sentence negative, place the word **no** (*not*) before the verb.

EXAMPLES:	**No hablo italiano.**	*I don't speak Italian.*
	No trabajo en el banco.	*I don't work in the bank.*
	No estudio inglés.	*I don't study English.*
	No compro en el mercado.	*I don't buy at the market.*
PRACTICE:	**Tra-BA-jo.**	*I work.*
	No tra-BA-jo.	*I don't work.*

 ## 6.1 WHERE PEOPLE WORK

ruso	*Russian (masc.)*	**Trabajo.**	*I work.*
rusa	*Russian (fem.)*	**No trabajo.**	*I don't work.*
eso	*that*	**¿Trabaja usted?**	*Do you work?*
ridículo(a)	*ridiculous*	**¿Trabajas tú?**	*Do you work? (fam.)*
Eso es ridículo.	*That is*	**No hablo…**	*I don't speak…*
	ridiculous.	**No compro…**	*I don't buy…*
mucho(a)	*much, a lot*		

6.2 LISTENING EXERCISE

Repeat each sentence after your instructor says it, reading along in the book as you speak.

1. No hablo ruso.
2. No hablo italiano.
3. No hablo español en casa.
4. No compro gasolina en el banco.
5. No estudio ruso.
6. No estudio italiano.
7. No trabajo en el banco.
8. No trabajo en la tienda.

6.3 ORAL EXERCISE

Answer the following questions.

1. ¿Habla usted inglés?
2. ¿Habla usted italiano?
3. ¿Habla usted ruso?
4. ¿Habla usted español?
5. ¿Habla usted español en casa?
6. ¿Habla usted español en la clase?
7. ¿Habla usted ruso en la clase?
8. ¿Compra usted flores en el mercado?
9. ¿Compra usted flores en el banco?
10. ¿Estudia usted italiano?
11. ¿Estudia usted ruso?
12. ¿Trabaja usted en el banco?
13. ¿Trabaja usted en la tienda?
14. ¿Trabaja usted mucho?

Can you do this exercise with your book closed?

Note: Notice that in the previous exercise, all the verbs in the questions end in **-a**. All the verbs in the answers end in **-o**.

QUESTIONS		ANSWERS	
¿Habla...?	*Do you speak...?*	Hablo...	*I speak...*
¿Compra...?	*Do you buy...?*	Compro...	*I buy...*
¿Estudia?	*Do you study?*	Estudio.	*I study.*
¿Trabaja?	*Do you work?*	Trabajo.	*I work.*

This is because the questions use the **usted** (*you* formal) form of the present tense and the answers use the **yo** (*I*) form.

6.4 WORD BUILDER

Pronunciation: Changing English words that end in -ble into Spanish

Most Spanish words which end in -ble are similar to English words, so you already know many of them. Practice their Spanish pronunciation. Stress the next to the last syllable of these words, like this: **pro-BA-ble.**

List of **-ble** words in Spanish (optional)

flexible	inevitable	noble	responsable
horrible	invisible	posible	terrible
imposible	irresistible	probable	visible

Spelling

The letter **s** is never doubled in Spanish. *Possible* is spelled **posible** and *impossible* is spelled **imposible**. Also, remember that **responsable** ends in **-able** in Spanish and in **-ible** in English. Don't forget that the **h** is silent in Spanish.

6.5 REVIEW–MINI-TEST

Close your book and write in Spanish the English words your instructor says.

1. terrible	5. possible	9. invisible
2. horrible	6. impossible	10. irresistible
3. noble	7. inevitable	11. visible
4. probable	8. flexible	12. responsible

📼 6.6 EVERYDAY EXPRESSIONS

Es grande.	*It's big.*	Es personal.	*It's personal.*
No es grande.	*It isn't big.*	Es probable.	*It's probable.*
Es posible.	*It's possible.*	No es probable.	*It's not probable.*
No es posible.	*It isn't possible.*	Es conveniente.	*It's convenient.*
Es imposible.	*It's impossible.*	No es	
Es importante.	*It's important.*	conveniente.	*It isn't convenient.*
No es	*It isn't important.*	Es horrible.	*It's horrible.*
importante.		Es diferente.	*It's different.*
Es terrible.	*It's terrible.*	Es natural.	*It's natural.*
Es excelente.	*It's excellent.*	Eso es diferente.	*That's different.*

6.7 ORAL EXERCISE

For each item indicated, give a reaction using the word provided. Follow the examples.

EXAMPLE: **una sopa de violetas / horrible**
ANSWER: **¡Es horrible!**

EXAMPLE: **una sopa de violetas / excelente**
ANSWER: **¡No es excelente!**

1. un auto / grande
2. un autobús / chiquito
3. un auto en la clase / posible
4. un avión en la clase / imposible
5. una rosa / natural
6. una fábrica / natural
7. un hospital en el centro / conveniente
8. mucho tráfico en el cento / conveniente
9. un despacho en casa / conveniente
10. una estatua en un museo / probable

📼 6.8 EXOTIC ANIMALS

el gorila	*the gorilla*
el león	*the lion*
el tigre	*the tiger*
su clase	*your class*

mi clase	*my class*
¡Gracias a Dios!	*Thank God!*
¡Ja, ja, ja!	*Ha, ha, ha!*
la India	*India**
África	*Africa*

***Note**: In Spanish, we say **la India** instead of *India*.

6.9 ORAL EXERCISE

Answer the following questions.

1. ¿Hay elefantes en África?
2. ¿Hay tigres en la India?
3. ¿Hay gorilas en México?
4. ¿Hay leones en Puerto Rico?
5. ¿Hay un elefante en su clase?
6. ¿Hay un tigre en su casa?
7. ¿Hay un león en su clase?
8. ¿Hay un gorila en su casa?

Grammar Summary: Using the present tense of **-ar** verbs (singular)

Very important: When you speak about one person (other than yourself), end the verb in -a.

EXAMPLES:

María estudia.	*María studies.*
El doctor trabaja.	*The doctor works.*
Roberto habla español.	*Roberto speaks Spanish.*
El conductor trabaja en el tren.	*The conductor works on the train.*
Mi papá trabaja mucho.	*My dad works a lot (much).*

When you address someone, end the verb in **-a** or **-as** depending on whether you have a familiar or polite relationship with the person you're addressing.

EXAMPLES: **Tú estudias.**   *You study. (fam.)*

Tú hablas español.   *You speak Spanish. (fam.)*

Tú trabajas.   *You work. (fam.)*

Usted estudia.   *You study. (polite)*

Usted habla italiano. *You speak Italian. (polite)*

Usted trabaja.   *You work. (polite)*

When you speak of yourself, end the verb in **-o**.

EXAMPLES: **Hablo…**   *I speak…*

Compro…   *I buy…*

Trabajo…   *I work…*

This is true of every single regular **-ar** verb in the Spanish language.

6.10 CONVERSATION VOCABULARY

¿Dónde?	*Where?*	**¿Dónde trabajas?**	*Where do you work? (fam.)*
el hospital	*hospital*		
el banco	*bank*	**¿Dónde trabaja Roberto?**	*Where does Roberto work?*
la fábrica	*factory*		
el despacho	*office*	**¿Dónde trabaja María?**	*Where does María work?*
¿Dónde trabaja usted?	*Where do you work?*		

📼 6.11 CONVERSATION

The instructor will point out groups of two students who will go to the front of the room and have a conversation about who works where.

Ask as many questions as you can. Your partner will answer them. Keep the conversation lively. When you have run out of questions you can ask easily, other students will take over. Ask at least four questions. Tell where your own friends work. Use the names of your friends or members of your family.

The following block will serve as a guide for your conversation. However, do not restrict yourself only to what is in the block.

Asking and telling where people work

FIRST STUDENT: ¿Dónde trabaja Sean?
SECOND STUDENT: Sean trabaja en un hotel.

FIRST STUDENT: ¿Dónde trabaja Kelly?
SECOND STUDENT: Kelly trabaja en un garaje.

FIRST STUDENT: ¿Dónde trabaja Sam?
SECOND STUDENT: Sam trabaja en un teatro.

FIRST STUDENT: ¿Dónde trabaja Heather?
SECOND STUDENT: Heather trabaja en un restaurante.

FIRST STUDENT: ¿Dónde trabaja Sandra?
SECOND STUDENT: Sandra trabaja en un museo.

FIRST STUDENT: ¿Dónde trabaja Jim?
SECOND STUDENT: Jim trabaja en una estación de gasolina.

6.12 READING EXERCISE: ¿DÓNDE TRABAJA?

In this lesson, you've learned to talk about the places where people work. Now look at the following ads for jobs. See if you can figure out where the people hired for each position will work, matching the ad to the place of employment below.

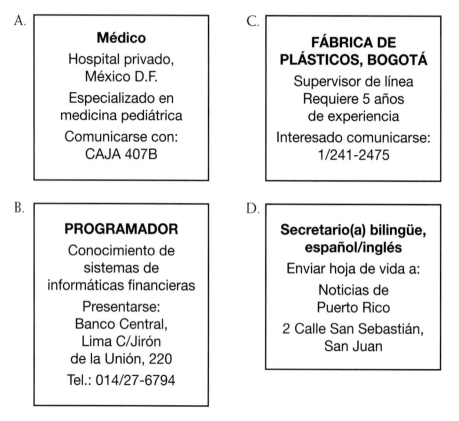

A.

Médico

Hospital privado,
México D.F.

Especializado en
medicina pediátrica

Comunicarse con:
CAJA 407B

B.

PROGRAMADOR

Conocimiento de
sistemas de
informáticas financieras

Presentarse:
Banco Central,
Lima C/Jirón
de la Unión, 220

Tel.: 014/27-6794

C.

**FÁBRICA DE
PLÁSTICOS, BOGOTÁ**

Supervisor de línea
Requiere 5 años
de experiencia

Interesado comunicarse:
1/241-2475

D.

**Secretario(a) bilingüe,
español/inglés**

Enviar hoja de vida a:

Noticias de
Puerto Rico

2 Calle San Sebastián,
San Juan

Where will they work? Match the ad with the place of employment.

_____ 1. una fábrica de plásticos en Bogotá, Colombia

_____ 2. un hospital en la ciudad de México

_____ 3. un banco en Lima, Perú

_____ 4. un despacho en San Juan, Puerto Rico

6.13 WRITING EXERCISE

Use your answers from Exercise 6.12 to write eight complete sentences, saying where people in each of the four professions advertised work and don't work.

EXAMPLE: **El médico trabaja en un(a)… .**
El médico no trabaja en un(a)… .

VOCABULARY

NOUNS

África	*Africa*	**la India**	*India*
el banco	*bank*	**el león**	*lion*
el despacho	*office*	**el ruso**	*Russian (language and person)*
la fábrica	*factory*		
el gorila	*gorilla*	**el tigre**	*tiger*
el hospital	*hospital*		

ADJECTIVES

ridículo(a)   *ridiculous*

VERBS

trabajar   *to work*

OTHER WORDS AND EXPRESSIONS

¿Dónde?	*Where?*	**Eso es diferente.**	*That's different.*
Es conveniente.	*It's convenient.*	**Eso es ridículo.**	*That's ridiculous.*
Es diferente.	*It's different.*	**¡Gracias a Dios!**	*Thank God!*
Es excelente.	*It's excellent.*	**¡Ja, ja, ja!**	*Ha, ha, ha!*
Es grande.	*It's big.*	**mi**	*my*
Es horrible.	*It's horrible.*	**mucho(a)**	*much, a lot*
Es importante.	*It's important.*	**No es conveniente.**	*It's not convenient.*
Es imposible.	*It's impossible.*		
Es natural.	*It's natural.*	**No es grande.**	*It's isn't big.*
Es personal.	*It's personal.*	**No es importante.**	*It's not important.*
Es posible.	*It's possible.*		
Es probable.	*It's probable.*	**No es posible.**	*It's not possible.*
Es terrible.	*It's terrible.*	**No es probable.**	*It's not probable.*
eso	*that*	**su**	*your*

OPTIONAL LIST

ADJECTIVES

flexible
horrible
imposible
inevitable
invisible
irresistible
noble
posible
probable
responsable
terrible
visible

LESSON 7

✺

Hablamos por teléfono

- The present tense of regular **-ar** verbs (singular and plural forms)
- Uses of **nada**
- Meanings of the **usted** form in the present tense
- Using the telephone
- More **-ar** verbs in Spanish

Grammar: Present tense of regular -ar verbs

To form the present tense of regular -ar verbs, remove the -ar, and add the following endings:

-o	-amos
-as	-áis
-a	-an

hablar *to speak, to talk*			
I speak	**hablo**	**hablamos**	*we speak*
you speak (fam.)	**hablas**	**habláis**	*you speak (pl. fam.)*
you speak (formal)		**hablan**	*you speak (pl. formal)*
he speaks			*they speak*
she speaks	**habla**		
it speaks			

*Note: The use of the second person plural familiar verb form (**habláis, nadáis**) varies from country to country. It is called the **vosotros** form and is used mostly in Spain to express the plural of **tú** (second person singular familiar). In most of Latin America, the third person plural verb form (**hablan, nadan**) is used to express the plural of **tú**. You don't need to learn this form, but you should be familiar with its use and able to recognize it.

nadar *to swim*			
I swim	**nado**	**nadamos**	*we swim*
you swim (fam.)	**nadas**	**nadáis**	*you swim (pl. fam.)*
you swim (formal)		**nadan**	*you swim (pl. formal)*
he swims			*they swim*
she swims	**nada**		
it swims			

preparar *to prepare*			
I prepare	**preparo**	**preparamos**	*we prepare*
you prepare (fam.)	**preparas**	**preparáis**	*you prepare (pl. fam.)*
you prepare (formal)		**preparan**	*you prepare (pl. formal)*
he prepares			*they prepare*
she prepares	**prepara**		
it prepares			

Repeat after your teacher: **hablo, hablas, habla, hablamos, hablan; nado, nadas, nada, nadamos, nadan.** Stress these verbs like this: **HA-blo, HA-blas, ha-BLA-mos, HA-blan; NA-do, NA-das, na-DA-mos, NA-dan.**

Grammar: Present tense endings of all regular -ar verbs

Every single **-ar** verb (regular) in the Spanish language ends in the letters below in the present tense. Learn these endings.

I	-o	-amos	*we*
you (fam.)	-as	-áis	*you (pl. fam.)*
you (formal)		-an	*you (pl. formal)*
he			*they*
she	-a		
it			

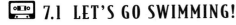 **7.1 LET'S GO SWIMMING!**

mexicano(a)	*Mexican*	**la piscina**	*swimming pool*
el mar	*sea*	**inmenso(a)**	*immense*
Nado.	*I swim.*	**el cielo**	*sky*
Nadamos.	*We swim.*	**Nadan.**	*They swim.*
Trabajamos.	*We work.*	**Trabajan.**	*They work.*

7.2 LISTENING EXERCISE

Repeat each sentence after your instructor says it, reading along in the book as you speak.

1. Nado en el mar.
2. Nado en la piscina.
3. Hablamos español en la clase.
4. No hablamos italiano en la clase.
5. No hablamos ruso en la clase.
6. Hablamos mucho.
7. Estudiamos mucho.
8. Estudiamos español en la clase.
9. Trabajamos mucho.
10. Los italianos hablan italiano.
11. Los rusos hablan ruso.
12. Los mexicanos hablan español.
13. El mar es inmenso.
14. El cielo es inmenso.

Spelling

Remember, words that express nationalities or languages do not begin with a capital letter.

7.3 ORAL EXERCISE

Answer the following questions.

EXAMPLE: **¿Hablamos español en la clase?**
ANSWER: **Sí, hablamos español en la clase.**

1. ¿Hablamos italiano en la clase?
2. ¿Hablamos ruso en la clase?
3. ¿Estudiamos español en la clase?
4. ¿Trabajamos mucho en la clase?
5. ¿Estudiamos italiano en la clase?
6. ¿Estudiamos ruso en la clase?
7. ¿Hablan español los mexicanos?
8. ¿Hablan italiano los italianos?

9. ¿Hablan ruso los rusos?   13. ¿Es grande la piscina?
10. ¿Hablan italiano los rusos? 14. ¿Dónde nada usted?
11. ¿Nada usted en el mar?   15. ¿Es grande el mar?
12. ¿Nada usted en la piscina?   16. ¿Es grande el cielo?

Can you do this exercise with your book closed?

Grammar: Uses of **nada**

nada	*nothing, not at all*	**No nada nada.**	*You (form.) don't swim at all.*
	He/She/It swims.		*He doesn't swim at all.*
	You (form.) swim.		*She doesn't swim at all.*
			It doesn't swim at all.

Repeat the following sentences, focusing on the word **nada**.

¿Qué preparamos para la cena?   *What are we making for dinner?*
Nada.   *Nothing.*

7.4 ORAL EXERCISE

Your instructor will ask individual students to change the following verbs into the *we* form (first person plural).

EXAMPLE: **estudiar**   ANSWER: **estudiamos**

1. comprar   3. progresar   5. hablar
2. nadar   4. trabajar   6. preparar

7.5 ORAL EXERCISE

Your instructor will ask individual students to change the following verbs into the they form (third person plural).

EXAMPLE: **estudiar**   ANSWER: **estudian**

1. hablar   3. preparar   5. progresar
2. trabajar   4. nadar   6. comprar

Grammar: Eight uses of the **usted / él / ella** form

The second person (formal) and third person (singular) of verbs may be used to express both questions and answers.

Canta.	*You sing.*	**¿Canta?**	*Do you sing?*
	He sings.		*Does he sing?*
	She sings.		*Does she sing?*
	It sings.		*Does it sing?*
Nada.	*You swim.*	**¿Nada?**	*Do you swim?*
	He swims.		*Does he swim?*
	She swims.		*Does she swim?*
	It swims.		*Does it swim?*

Therefore **Canta mucho/¿Canta mucho?** can mean eight things.

1. You sing a lot.
2. He sings a lot.
3. She sings a lot.
4. It sings a lot.

5. Do you sing a lot?
6. Does he sing a lot?
7. Does she sing a lot?
8. Does it sing a lot?

7.6 NUMBERS

número	*number*	seis	*six*
cero	*zero*	siete	*seven*
uno	*one*	ocho	*eight*
dos	*two*	nueve	*nine*
tres	*three*	diez	*ten*
cuatro	*four*	once	*eleven*
cinco	*five*	doce	*twelve*

7.7 ORAL EXERCISE

Repeat these phone numbers aloud after your instructor says them.

1. 321-5214   tres dos uno, cinco dos uno cuatro
2. 212-3202   dos uno dos, tres dos cero dos
3. 534-1234   cinco tres cuatro, uno dos tres cuatro
4. 345-1234   tres cuatro cinco, uno dos tres cuatro
5. 123-4567   uno dos tres, cuatro cinco seis siete
6. 890-6789   ocho nueve cero, seis siete ocho nueve
7. 234-5678   dos tres cuatro, cinco seis siete ocho

7.8 CONVERSATION VOCABULARY

Oye.	*Listen. (fam.)*
¿Cuál?	*Which? (What?)*
¿Cuál es?	*Which (What) is it?*

el número de teléfono	*telephone number*
el número de teléfono de Susan	*Susan's phone number*
¿Cuál es su número de teléfono?	*What (Which) is your phone number? What (Which) is his phone number? What (Which) is her phone number?*
Bueno.	*Good. Hello (when answering the phone in many Spanish-speaking countries).*
Muchas gracias.	*Thank you very much. Many thanks.*
Adiós.	*Good-bye.*
¿Quién?	*Who?*
¿Quién habla?	*Who speaks? Who is speaking?*
Habla María.	*María speaks. María is speaking.*
Un momento.	*Just a moment.*

 ## 7.9 CONVERSATION

Form groups of two students and conduct a phone conversation. Change the name and the numbers in the conversation if you wish.

The following block will serve as a guide for your conversation. However, do not restrict yourself only to what is in the block.

Talking on the telephone

FIRST STUDENT: Bueno.

SECOND STUDENT: Bueno. ¿Quién habla?

FIRST STUDENT: (Say your own name).

SECOND STUDENT: Buenos días, (classmate's name). Habla (say your own name). ¿Cómo estás?

FIRST STUDENT: Bien, gracias. ¿Y tú?

SECOND STUDENT: Bien, gracias. Oye, ¿cuál es el número de teléfono de Susana?

FIRST STUDENT: Un momento… su número es ocho uno dos, tres cuatro seis siete.

SECOND STUDENT: Muchas gracias, (name). Adiós.

FIRST STUDENT: Adiós, (name).

7.10 WORD BUILDER

The following -ar verbs are similar to English words.

List of -ar verbs in Spanish (optional)

abandonar	causar	galopar
aceptar	comparar	importar
adaptar	conectar	inspirar
admirar	consultar	necesitar
adoptar	conversar	representar
adorar	declarar	trotar
afectar	exportar	usar
ajustar	expresar	
alarmar	flotar	

7.11 READING EXERCISE: LA GUÍA DE TELÉFONO

In this lesson, you learned how to conduct a telephone conversation. Many of the words used to describe different types of phone calls and services are cognates. Look at the following page from a U.S. telephone directory that describes in Spanish the services provided by the phone company. Then answer the questions that follow.

Páginas en español

Teléfonos de Emergencia	C3	Facturación y Pagos	C21
Estableciendo Servicio	C4	Llamadas de Larga Distancia	C24
Catálogo de Servicio	C9	Llamadas Internacionales	C31
Servicio de Directorio y Asistencia de Directorio	C18	Información y Derechos del Consumidor	C32
Llamadas con Ayuda de la Operadora	C19		

la página	*the page*
estableciendo	*establishing*
la llamada	*the phone call*
la ayuda	*the help, assistance*
el derecho	*the right*

1. On what page can you find information about making long distance calls?
2. On what page can you find out how to establish telephone service?
3. On what page can you get information about consumer rights?
4. On what page can you find a list of services?
5. On what page can you find emergency telephone numbers?
6. On what page can you find information about directory services and directory assistance?
7. On what page can you find out how to make an international call?
8. On what page can you find out how to make an operator-assisted call?

7.12 WRITING EXERCISE

Look at the directory of Spanish pages in the phone book on page 77. Now, write a conversation in which you are talking to a friend on the phone. She wants to call some of these departments, but this page is missing from her directory. Write a conversation from start to finish that includes the five phrases indicated. Use the conversation on page 76 of this lesson as an example.

Phrases: ¿Cuál es el número de teléfono de los teléfonos de emergencia?
...del catálogo de servicio...
...del servicio de directorio y asistencia de directorio...
...de las llamadas internacionales...
En la página (*On page*) C3 hay un número de teléfono para los teléfonos de emergencia.

VOCABULARY

NOUNS

el cielo	*sky*	el número	*number*
el mar	*sea*	la piscina	*pool*

VERBS

cantar	*to sing*
nadar	*to swim*
preparar	*to prepare*

ADJECTIVES

cero	*zero*	ocho	*eight*
uno	*one*	nueve	*nine*
dos	*two*	diez	*ten*
tres	*three*	once	*eleven*
cuatro	*four*	doce	*twelve*
cinco	*five*	inmenso(a)	*immense*
seis	*six*	mexicano	*mexican*
siete	*seven*		

OTHR WORDS AND EXPRESSIONS

Adiós.	*Good-bye.*	el número de teléfono	*telephone number*
Bueno.	*Good. Hello*	Habla (person).	*[Person] speaking.*
¿Cuál?	*Which, what?*	Muchas gracias.	*Thank you very much.*
¿Cuál es?	*Which (What) is it?*		*Many thanks.*
¿Cuál es su número de teléfono?	*What (Which) is your telephone number?*	nada	*nothing, not at all*
		Oye.	*Listen.*
el número de teléfono de (nombre)	*the telephone number of (name)*	¿Quién?	*Who?*
		¿Quién habla?	*Who is speaking?*
		Un momento.	*Just a moment.*

OPTIONAL LIST

VERBS

abandonar
aceptar
adaptar
admirar
adoptar
adorar
afectar
ajustar
alarmar
causar
comparar
conectar
consultar

conversar
declarar
exportar
expresar
flotar
galopar
importar
inspirar
necesitar
representar
trotar
usar

LESSON 8

❋

En casa

- The verb **estar** *(to be)*
- Asking and telling where people or things are located

Grammar: Using **estar** to express location

Whenever you say where a thing or person is, use the verb **estar**. Say these sentences:

El auto está en el garaje.   *The car is in the garage.*

El tren está en la estación.   *The train is in the station.*

Estar is used to describe location.

estar *to be*			
I am	estoy	estamos	*we are*
you are (fam.)	estás	estáis	*you are (pl. fam.)*
you are (formal)		están	*you are (pl. formal)*
he is	está		*they are*
she is			
it is			

Repeat the forms of this verb after your instructor says them in Spanish. This verb is very important. It is frequently used in Spanish conversation, as in the phrases **¿Cómo está?** and **¿Cómo estás?** that you have already learned.

Grammar: Irregular verbs

Notice that **estoy** (*I am*) doesn't end in **-o**. It ends in **-y**. This is because it is an irregular verb. Verbs that do not follow the regular present tense **-ar** forms are called irregular verbs.

8.1 ORAL EXERCISE

Your instructor will point to individual students who will say the forms of this verb. Repeat: **estoy, estás, está, estamos, están.**

8.2 THE HOUSE

la crema	cream	su	your (sing.), his, hers,
el sofá	sofa		its
la mesa	table	el paraguas	umbrella
en la mesa	on the table	¿Dónde está…?	Where is…?
la llave	key	¿Dónde están…?	Where are…?
No sé.	I don't know.	¿Dónde está	Where is my hat?
el azúcar	sugar	mi sombrero?	
la papa	potato	¿Dónde están	Where are the keys?
mamá	mother, Mom	las llaves?	
papá	father, Dad	el tomate	tomato
el estéreo	stereo	el dinero	money
mi	my	muchísimo(a)	very, very much

Note: **Para** means *for*, **aguas** means *waters*. **Paraguas** literally means *for waters*, although it is the Spanish word for *umbrella*. In English, we have the word **parasol**, which means *for sun* in Spanish.

8.3 LISTENING EXERCISE

Repeat each sentence after your instructor says it, reading along in the book as you speak.

1. La crema está en la mesa.
2. El café está en la mesa.
3. El plato está en la mesa.
4. Mi sombrero está en el sofá.
5. Las flores están en la mesa.
6. El disco compacto está en el estéreo.
7. ¿Dónde está mi sombrero?
8. ¿Dónde está la llave?
9. La llave está en la mesa.
10. El dinero está en el banco.
11. La ensalada está en el plato.
12. ¿Habla usted español?
13. Hablamos español en la clase.
14. Las papas están en la mesa.
15. Los tomates están en la mesa.

8.4 ORAL EXERCISE

Answer the following questions.

EXAMPLE: ¿Dónde está usted? (clase de español)
ANSWER: Estoy en la clase de español.

1. ¿Dónde está el profesor? (clase)
2. ¿Dónde está el doctor? (hospital)
3. ¿Dónde está el café? (mesa)
4. ¿Dónde está el plato? (mesa)
5. ¿Dónde está la crema? (mesa)
6. ¿Dónde está el conductor? (tren)
7. ¿Dónde está María? (banco)
8. ¿Dónde está su sombrero? (en casa)
9. ¿Dónde está el disco compacto? (estéreo)
10. ¿Dónde está la llave? (mesa)
11. ¿Dónde están las flores? (mesa)
12. ¿Dónde están los estudiantes? (clase)
13. ¿Dónde están las peras? (mesa)
14. ¿Dónde está su mamá? (en casa) ¿Y su papá? (banco)
15. ¿Dónde están las aspirinas? (¡No sé!)
16. ¿Dónde están las blusas? (¡No sé!)
17. ¿Dónde está el paraguas? (¡No sé!)

8.5 ORAL OR WRITTEN EXERCISE

Use estoy, estás, está, estamos, or están to complete the following sentences.

EXAMPLE: Yo ... en la clase.
ANSWER: Yo estoy en la clase.

1. Tú ... en la casa.
2. Las papas ... en la mesa.
3. La crema ... en la mesa.
4. Yo ... en la clase.
5. El tren ... en la estación.
6. El actor ... en el teatro.
7. Nosotros ... en la clase.
8. Roberto y María no ... en el banco.
9. Las flores ... en la mesa.
10. Nosotras ... en la clase de español.
11. La ensalada ... en el plato.
12. Tú ... enfrente de la casa.

8.6 ORAL EXERCISE

Answer the following questions.

1. ¿Dónde está su profesor de español?
2. ¿Dónde está su estéreo?
3. ¿Habla usted español?
4. ¿Nada usted en el mar?
5. ¿Estudia usted mucho?
6. ¿Es famoso su papá?
7. ¿Hay flores en el parque?

8. ¿Dónde está su mamá?
9. ¿Dónde están sus llaves?
10. ¿Hablamos español en la clase?
11. ¿Dónde está su paraguas?
12. ¿Dónde están los estudiantes?
13. ¿Dónde está el disco compacto?
14. ¿Dónde está su papá?

8.7 COMPOSITION VOCABULARY

Tienen…	*They have…*	fantástico(a)	*fantastic*
el jardín	*garden*	también	*also*
más	*more*	la playa	*beach*

todos	everybody	elegante	elegant (masc., fem.)
el agua	water	la ciudad	city
el Océano Pacífico	the Pacific Ocean	azul, azul	very blue

8.8 LISTENING EXERCISE

Listen to the following composition as your instructor reads it aloud. Read along in your book, paying particular attention to the pronunciation of the Spanish words.

México

En México hay casas muy bonitas y edificios modernos. Unas casas tienen jardines grandes. En los jardines hay muchas flores. Hay rosas blancas y rosas rojas. Hay violetas, tulipanes, geranios y más.

En México también hay montañas grandes. Las montañas son fantásticas. Hay playas extraordinarias y hoteles y restaurantes muy elegantes. En las playas hay muchos turistas americanos y mexicanos. Todos nadan.

El agua es transparente, fresca y azul, azul. Acapulco, una ciudad mexicana, tiene una playa muy famosa. Está en el Océano Pacífico.

8.9 ORAL EXERCISE (OPTIONAL)

Your instructor will point to individual students who will read one sentence in the above composition and translate it into English.

8.10 READING EXERCISE

Now read aloud a whole paragraph of the composition. Try to read as smoothly as you can.

8.11 ORAL OR WRITTEN MINI-TEST

Answer the following questions to see how well you have understood the composition.

1. ¿Hay casas bonitas en México?
2. ¿Hay muchas flores en los jardines?
3. ¿Hay rosas rojas?
4. ¿Hay pinos en los jardines?

5. ¿Hay montañas grandes en México?

6. ¿Cómo son las montañas?

7. ¿Está Acapulco en el Océano Atlántico?

8. ¿Hay turistas en las playas?

9. ¿Es fresca el agua?

10. ¿Es verde el agua?

8.12 CONVERSATION

Form groups of two students and ask each other where different things are. The following block will serve as a guide for your conversation. However, do not restrict yourself only to what is in the block.

Asking and telling where people or things are

FIRST STUDENT: ¿Dónde está el café?
SECOND STUDENT: El café está en la mesa.
FIRST STUDENT: ¿Dónde está la crema?
SECOND STUDENT: La crema está en la mesa.

FIRST STUDENT: ¿Dónde está el doctor?
SECOND STUDENT: El doctor está en el hospital.
FIRST STUDENT: ¿Dónde está el actor?
SECOND STUDENT: El actor está en el teatro.

FIRST STUDENT: ¿Dónde están los estudiantes?
SECOND STUDENT: Los estudiantes están en la clase.
FIRST STUDENT: ¿Dónde está la llave?
SECOND STUDENT: La llave está en la mesa.

FIRST STUDENT: ¿Dónde está el azúcar?
SECOND STUDENT: El azúcar está en la mesa.
FIRST STUDENT: ¿Dónde está el paraguas?
SECOND STUDENT: No sé.

FIRST STUDENT: ¿Dónde está Bernardo?
SECOND STUDENT: Bernardo está en el banco.
FIRST STUDENT: ¿Dónde está su papá?
SECOND STUDENT: Mi papá está en su despacho.

FIRST STUDENT: ¿Dónde están los chocolates?
SECOND STUDENT: Los chocolates están en la mesa.
FIRST STUDENT: ¿Dónde está el presidente?
SECOND STUDENT: El presidente está en Washington.

8.13 READING EXERCISE: CASAS EN ALQUILER

In this lesson you learned about houses and location. Here are three ads for rental houses in La Plata, Argentina. Look at the ads, then answer the questions that follow.

CASA A

Código: **019 - 8076**	Precio: **alquiler $ 320**
Tipo: **casa**	
Dirección: **10 bis e/ 84 y 85**	Localidad: **La Plata**

Información Detallada

dormitorios: **2**	liv/com/coc: **coc, liv-com**
baños: **1**	pileta: **no**
garaje: **sí**	agua corriente: **sí**
antigüedad: **1**	patio: **sí**
gas natural: **sí**	

observaciones: casa ubicada en barrio nuevo, próximo a barrio Monasterio, todos los servicios (gas y luz).

CASA B

Código: **027 - 7376**	Precio: **alquiler $ 380**
Tipo: **casa**	
Dirección: **4 y 35 PB**	Localidad: **La Plata**
Información Detallada	
dormitorios: **2**	liv/com/coc: **coc, liv-com**
baños: **1**	pileta: **no**
garaje: **no**	agua corriente: **sí**
antigüedad: **40**	patio: **sí**
gas natural: **sí**	

observaciones: patio chico con parrilla

CASA C

Código: **022 - 9205**	Precio: **alquiler $ 1000**
Tipo: **casa**	
Dirección: **34 e/ 8 y 9**	Localidad: **La Plata**
Información Detallada	
dormitorios: **3**	liv/com/coc: **liv-com, coc-com**
baños: **3**	pileta: **sí**
garaje: **sí**	agua corriente: **sí**
antigüedad: **5**	patio: **sí**
gas natural: **sí**	

observaciones: muy equipada, excelente estado

First, see if you can figure out what some of the words in the ads mean by completing the following matching exercise. Look back at the ads and find the words to help you guess their meaning.

1. liv-com (living-comedor)
2. agua corriente
3. gas natural
4. antigüedad
5. alquiler

a. *natural gas*
b. *living-dining room*
c. *rent*
d. *running water*
e. *age*

Now answer the following questions about the ads.

1. ¿Qué casa tiene un alquiler de $1000?
2. ¿Qué casa tiene un alquiler de $320?
3. ¿Qué casa tiene tres dormitorios *(bedrooms)*?
4. ¿Qué casa tiene una pileta *(pool)*?
5. ¿Qué casas tienen patio?
6. ¿Qué casa es vieja *(old)*?

8.14 WRITING EXERCISE

Now, using the ads in Exercise 8.13 as models, write a similar ad for a house. It may be the house you grew up in, the house you are living in now, or an imaginary house. Use the words from Exercise 8.13 and follow the models.

Useful words: **baño** *(bathroom)*, **cocina** *(kitchen)*, **dormitorios, garaje, patio, pileta/piscina, sala/living** *(living room)*, **comedor, grande, chico**

VOCABULARY

NOUNS

el agua	*water*	**el jardín**	*garden*
el azúcar	*sugar*	**la llave**	*key*
la ciudad	*city*	**mamá**	*mother, Mom*
la crema	*cream*	**el Océano Pacífico**	*the Pacific Ocean*
el dinero	*money*		
el estéreo	*stereo*	**papá**	*father, Dad*

la papa	*potato*	todos	*everybody*
el paraguas	*umbrella*	el tomate	*tomato*
la playa	*beach*	la mesa	*table*
el sofá	*sofa*		

VERBS

estar	*to be (located)*

ADJECTIVES

azul, azul	*very blue*
elegante	*elegant (masc., fem.)*
fantástico(a)	*fantastic*

OTHER WORDS AND EXPRESSIONS

¿Dónde está…?	*Where is…?*	muchísimo(a)	*very, very much*
¿Dónde están…?	*Where are…?*	No sé.	*I don't know.*
en la mesa	*on the table*	su	*Your (sing.), his, her, its*
más	*more*	también	*also*
mi	*my*	Tienen…	*They have…*

LESSON 9

¡Vamos todos!
- The verb **ir** *(to go)*
- **Al**
- **¿Dónde?** and **¿Adónde?**
- Days of the week
- Asking and telling destinations

Grammar: The verb **ir**

The verb **ir** (to go) is the most irregular verb in the Spanish language. It is also one of the most important verbs. Remember this verb!

		ir *to go*		
I go, I'm going	**voy**	**vamos**	*we go, we're going*	
you go, you're going (fam.)	**vas**	**vais**	*you go, you're going (pl. fam.)*	
you go, you're going (formal) *he goes, he's going* *she goes, she's going* *it goes, it's going*	**va**	**van**	*you go, you're going (pl. formal)* *they go, they're going*	

EXAMPLES: —**Voy a la fiesta ¿Y tú?**   *I'm going to the party. And you?*

              —**No voy, pero Mario va.**   *I'm not going, but Mario is going.*

9.1 ORAL EXERCISE

Your instructor will point to students who will give the forms of **ir** (to go). Study these forms until you know them without the slightest doubt.

Remember that you frequently drop the words **yo**, **usted**, etc., with a conjugated verb (a verb not in the infinitive form).

📼 9.2 GET ORGANIZED!

a	to	el gimnasio	gymnasium
a la	to the (fem.)	esta	this
al	to the (masc.)	la tarde	afternoon
la fiesta	party	esta tarde	this afternoon
el aeropuerto	airport	esta noche	tonight
mañana	tomorrow	en avión	by plane
la mañana	the morning	en tren	by train
el concierto	concert	el fútbol	soccer game, soccer

Grammar: Forming **al**

Contraction:	**a**	+	**el**	=	**al**
	(to)		*(the)*		*(to the)*

Al forms a contraction with the masculine definite article **el** only.

  EXAMPLE: **Voy** *al* **teatro**, but **voy** *a la* **fiesta**.

📼 9.3 LISTENING EXERCISE

Repeat each sentence after your instructor says it, reading along in the book as you speak.

1. Voy a la fiesta mañana.
2. Voy a la clase mañana.
3. No voy al cine mañana.
4. Voy al teatro mañana.
5. No voy a México mañana.
6. Voy al parque esta tarde.

7. Voy al cine esta tarde.
8. Voy al mercado esta tarde.
9. Voy al banco esta tarde.
10. Voy a México en avión.
11. Voy al aeropuerto.
12. No voy al parque.
13. No voy a la tienda.
14. Voy a la fiesta esta noche.

9.4 ORAL EXERCISE

Answer the following questions.

EXAMPLE: ¿**Va al cine?**
ANSWER: **Sí, voy al cine esta tarde. (No, no voy al cine.)**

1. ¿Va a la fiesta?
2. ¿Va a la clase mañana?
3. ¿Va a Puerto Rico?
4. ¿Va al parque?
5. ¿Va al mercado mañana?
6. ¿Va al banco esta tarde?
7. ¿Va a México?
8. ¿Va al gimnasio mañana?
9. ¿Va al teatro mañana?
10. ¿Va al teatro esta noche?

Can you do this exercise with your book closed?

Grammar: Using **vamos**

Vamos means *we go, we are going,* and *let's go.*

   EXAMPLE: ¡**Vamos a la playa!**   *Let's go to the beach!*
                                        We're going to the beach!

9.5 LISTENING EXERCISE

Repeat each sentence after your instructor says it, reading along in the book as you speak.

1. ¡Vamos!
2. ¡Vamos al cine!
3. ¡Vamos al parque!
4. ¡Vamos al teatro!
5. ¡Vamos a la playa!
6. ¡Vamos a la fiesta!

9.6 ORAL OR WRITTEN EXERCISE

Answer the following questions.

1. ¿Va la profesora a la clase esta tarde?
2. ¿Va Ud. al banco esta tarde?
3. ¿Va su mamá a México?
4. ¿Va su papá a la fiesta mañana?
5. ¿Va Ud. al parque esta tarde?
6. ¿Van los turistas al aeropuerto en taxi?
7. ¿Nada usted en la piscina?
8. ¿Habla usted español?
9. ¿Hablamos italiano en la clase de español?
10. ¿Hablan ruso en Rusia?
11. ¿Dónde están sus llaves?
12. ¿Dónde están los estudiantes de español?
13. ¿Dónde está el paraguas?
14. ¿Hay flores en su casa?

Grammar: ¿**Adónde?** and ¿**Dónde?**

When you use any form of the verb **ir** *(to go)* in a question, use ¿**Adónde?**

Remember: ¿**Dónde?** means *Where?*

¿**Adónde?** means *To where?*

Always use ¿**Adónde?** when you ask a question about a destination with any form of the verb **ir**.

EXAMPLES: ¿**Adónde va? Voy al teatro.**

¿**Adónde van? Van a la fiesta.**

9.7 THE DAYS OF THE WEEK

la semana	*week*	el lunes	*(on) Monday*
el día	*day*	el martes	*(on) Tuesday*
los días de la semana	*the days of the week*	el miércoles	*(on) Wednesday*
		el jueves	*(on) Thursday*
el fin de semana	*the weekend*	el viernes	*(on) Friday*
el domingo	*(on) Sunday*	el sábado	*(on) Saturday*

Note: In Spanish, the days of the week begin with lower case letters.

9.8 ORAL EXERCISE

Answer the following questions.

1. ¿Adónde vas el sábado?
2. ¿Adónde vas el domingo?
3. ¿Adónde vas el lunes?
4. ¿Adónde vas el martes?
5. ¿Adónde vas mañana?
6. ¿Adónde vas el jueves?
7. ¿Adónde vas el miércoles?
8. ¿Adónde vas el viernes?
9. ¿Dónde vas a nadar?
10. ¿Dónde vas a trabajar?
11. ¿Dónde vas a comprar frutas frescas?
12. ¿Dónde vas a estudiar?
13. ¿Dónde vas a hablar español?
14. ¿Dónde vas a comprar discos compactos?

Can you do this exercise with your book closed?

9.9 CONVERSATION VOCABULARY

Ven.	*Come. (fam.)*	**Es una idea**	*It's an excellent idea.*
Ven acá.	*Come here. (fam.)*	**excelente.**	
Mira.	*Look. (fam.)*	**Está estudiando.**	*He/She is studying.*
¿Verdad?	*Isn't that so (true)?*	**Está jugando**	*He/She is playing tennis.*
¡Qué bueno!	*Great! (How good!)*	**tenis.**	
allí	*there*	**Está jugando**	*He/She is playing*
Allí está Bárbara.	*There is Bárbara.*	**baloncesto.**	*basketball.*
el club	*the club*		

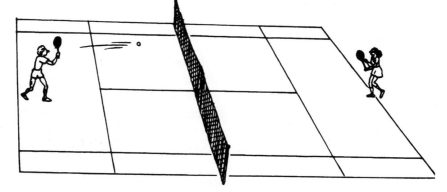

9.10 CONVERSATION

Form groups of three students each and conduct a conversation. To make things more interesting, talk about students you know and their activities.

The following block will serve as a guide for your conversation. However, do not restrict yourself only to what is in the block.

Talking about activities

FIRST STUDENT: Buenas tardes. ¿Cómo estás?

SECOND STUDENT: Bien, gracias. ¿Y tú?

FIRST STUDENT: Bien, gracias. Oye, ¿dónde está María?

SECOND STUDENT: Está en casa. Está estudiando.

FIRST STUDENT: María estudia mucho, ¿verdad?

SECOND STUDENT: Sí, estudia muchísimo. Progresa mucho en la clase de español.

FIRST STUDENT: Mira. Allí está (name of third student). (To third student) (¡Name!) Ven acá.

THIRD STUDENT: Buenas tardes. ¿Cómo están?

SECOND STUDENT: Bien gracias. ¿Y tú?

THIRD STUDENT:	Bien, gracias.
FIRST STUDENT:	Buenas tardes. ¿Dónde está Susana?
THIRD STUDENT:	Está jugando tenis en el club.
FIRST STUDENT:	¿Dónde está Bernardo?
SECOND STUDENT:	Está jugando fútbol en el parque.
THIRD STUDENT:	¿Dónde está Pedro?
SECOND STUDENT:	Está jugando baloncesto en el gimnasio.
FIRST STUDENT:	¿Vamos al parque?
SECOND STUDENT:	No, gracias.
THIRD STUDENT:	¿Vamos al club?
FIRST STUDENT:	No, gracias.
SECOND STUDENT:	¿Vamos al cine?
THIRD STUDENT:	Sí, ¡Qué bueno! Vamos al cine.
FIRST STUDENT:	Sí, vamos al cine. Es una idea excelente.

9.11 READING EXERCISE: LOS JAGUARES

The Jaguares are an internationally popular Mexican band. Look at their itinerary for the months of July through September of 2002, then answer the questions that follow.

Julio 11 jueves	Concierto Alicante, España - Invitados de Estopa
Julio 12 viernes	Festival Espárrago: Garbag, Iggy Pop, Bunbury, Dover, Orishas, Tabletón, Richie Hawtin, Amaral, Big Soul, El Barrio, Extremoduro, Fangoria, Antonio Orozco, Sidonie, Sôber, Tabletom, Jaguares y más…
Julio 13 sábado	Concierto Madrid: Fiesta Latina (Jaguares, Rabanes, Ratones Paranoicos)
Julio 17 miércoles	Concierto Madrid
Julio 18 jueves	Concierto Zaragoza
Julio 20 sábado	Concierto Barcelona
Julio 21 domingo	Concierto Getafe, España-Invitados de Estopa
Sept. 13 viernes	Revolución 2002 - Anaheim (Jaguares, Morrissey y más…) Arrowhead Pond
Sept. 14 sábado	Revolución 2002 - Berkeley - (Jaguares, Morrissey y más…) Greek Theater (Univ. de Berkeley)
Sept. 15 domingo	Revolución 2002 - San Diego - (Jaguares, Morrissey y más…) Open Air Theater SDSU (Campus de la Univ. de San Diego State)
Sept. 18 miércoles	Revolución 2002 - Denver - The Fillmore
Sept. 20 viernes	Revolución 2002 - Chicago
Sept. 21 sábado	Revolución 2002 - New York
Sept. 22 domingo	Revolución 2002 - Atlanta - The Tabernacle
Sept. 25 miércoles	Revolución 2002 - Miami - Billboard Live
Sept. 27 viernes	Revolución 2002 - Laredo - Civic Theater
Sept. 28 sábado	Revolución 2002 - Dallas - Bronco Bowl
Sept. 29 domingo	Revolución 2002 - San Antonio - Laurie Auditorium (Trinity University)

1. Usted está en Madrid, España. ¿Qué días de la semana es posible ir a un concierto de los Jaguares?
2. ¿Qué día van los Jaguares a Chicago?, ¿a Atlanta?, ¿a Miami?
3. ¿Qué otro artista está en concierto con los Jaguares en California los días 13 y 14 de septiembre?
4. ¿Qué día de la semana es el Festival Espárrago?, ¿y la Fiesta Latina en Madrid?

9.12 WRITING EXERCISE

What are your plans for the week ahead? Write a diary saying what you will do each day of the coming week, starting with Monday and ending with Sunday. Write complete sentences. Follow the example.

EXAMPLE: **El lunes voy a…**

VOCABULARY

NOUNS

el aeropuerto	*airport*	**lunes**	*Monday*
el baloncesto	*basketball*	**la mañana**	*morning*
el club	*club*	**martes**	*Tuesday*
el concierto	*concert*	**miércoles**	*Wednesday*
el día	*day*	**la noche**	*night*
domingo	*Sunday*	**sábado**	*Saturday*
la fiesta	*party*	**la semana**	*week*
el fútbol	*soccer game, soccer*	**la tarde**	*afternoon*
el fin de semana	*the weekend*	**el tenis**	*tennis*
el gimnasio	*gymnasium*	**viernes**	*Friday*
jueves	*Thursday*		

VERBS

ir	*to go*

OTHER WORDS AND EXPRESSIONS

a	*to*	**Está jugando baloncesto.**	*He/She is playing basketball.*
a la	*to the (fem.)*	**Está jugando tenis.**	*He/She is playing tennis.*
acá	*here*		
al	*to the (masc.)*		
allí	*there*	**esta noche**	*tonight*
Allí está…	*There's…*	**esta tarde**	*this afternoon*
el + *day of the week*	*on (day of the week)*	**mañana**	*tomorrow*
		Mira.	*Look. (fam.)*
en avión	*by plane*	**¡Qué bueno!**	*Great! (How good!)*
en tren	*by train*	**Vamos a…**	*Let's go (to)…*
Es una idea excelente.	*It's an excellent idea.*	**Ven.**	*Come. (fam.)*
		Ven acá.	*Come here. (fam.)*
Está estudiando.	*He/She is studying.*	**¿Verdad?**	*Isn't that so (true)?*

LESSON 10

¡Vamos a comprar ropa!
- Expressing the future with **ir** + **a** + infinitive
- Clothing
- Planning and talking about purchases

Grammar: Infinitives

The infinitive is the *to* form of the verb, such as *to swim, to buy*, etc. It is called an infinitive because until it is conjugated into a specific tense, it has no idea of time or subject attached to it.

10.1 LISTENING EXERCISE

Stress the last syllable of infinitives firmly, like this: **com-PRAR.**

1. comprar
2. hablar
3. estudiar
4. nadar
5. trabajar
6. depositar
7. estar

Grammar: Expressing the future with **ir**

To express the future, use forms of **ir**, plus the preposition **a**, before the infinitive that says what you are going to do.

EXAMPLES: **Voy a comprar...**   *I'm going to buy...*
                ¿Va a comprar...?   *Are you going to buy...?*

10.2 ORAL EXERCISE

Answer the following questions.

1. ¿Va a comprar pan en el mercado?
2. ¿Va a estudiar esta noche?
3. ¿Va a trabajar mañana?
4. ¿Va a hablar español en clase?
5. ¿Va a estar en casa el sábado?
6. ¿Va a nadar esta tarde?

Can you do this exercise with your book closed?

10.3 THE CLOTHING STORE

la falda	*skirt*	para...	*for...*
la corbata	*necktie*	¿Va a	*Are you going to buy...?*
el suéter	*sweater*	comprar...?	
el regalo	*present*	Voy a	*I'm going to buy...*
la bicicleta	*bicycle*	comprar...	
los zapatos	*shoes*	No voy a	*I'm not going to buy...*
para su papá	*for your father*	comprar...	
para mi mamá	*for my mother*	¿Va a estar...?	*Are you going to be...?*
la tienda de ropa	*the clothing store*		*(in a place)*

Punctuation

As you may have noticed, Spanish uses an upside down exclamation mark
(¡) before an exclamation.

EXAMPLE: **¡Qué bueno!**   *Great! How good!*

10.4 CONVERSATION VOCABULARY

¿Adónde vas?	*Where are you going? (fam.)*	**el jamón**	*ham*
el libro	*book*	**el televisor**	*television set*
¿Qué?	*What?*	**la casete, la cinta**	*cassette, tape*
¿Qué vas a comprar?	*What are you going to buy? (fam.)*	**el vestido**	*dress*
la camisa	*shirt*	**¿En qué puedo servirle?**	*How may I help you?*
la antena parabólica	*satellite dish*	**Quisiera...**	*I would like...*
		Necesito...	*I need...*
el chicle	*gum*	**¿Es todo?**	*Is that all?*

10.5 ORAL EXERCISE

With another student, take turns asking and answering the questions provided.

1. ¿Vas a comprar un televisor esta semana?

2. ¿Vas a comprar un libro esta semana?

3. ¿Qué vas a comprar para tu papá?

4. ¿Qué vas a comprar para tu mamá?

5. ¿Vas a trabajar mañana?

6. ¿Vas a ir a un restaurante mañana?

7. ¿Vas a ir al cine esta noche?

8. ¿Vas a jugar baloncesto en el gimnasio este domingo?

9. ¿Vas a comprar un libro para esta clase?

10. ¿Vas a estudiar esta noche?

11. ¿Vas a estar en casa esta noche?

12. ¿Vas a nadar mañana?

Can you do this exercise with your book closed?

10.6 CONVERSATION

Your instructor will point out two students who will ask each other what they are going to buy. Take turns asking and answering the questions.

The following block will serve as a guide for your conversation. However, do not restrict yourself only to what is in the block.

What are you going to buy?

FIRST STUDENT: ¿Adónde vas?
SECOND STUDENT: Voy al centro.

FIRST STUDENT: ¿Qué vas a comprar?
SECOND STUDENT: Voy a comprar una bicicleta.

FIRST STUDENT: ¿Vas a comprar un radio?
SECOND STUDENT: No. No voy a comprar un radio.

FIRST STUDENT: ¿Vas a comprar un disco compacto?
SECOND STUDENT: Sí. Voy a comprar un disco compacto.

FIRST STUDENT: ¿Vas a comprar unos libros?
SECOND STUDENT: Sí. voy a comprar unos libros.

FIRST STUDENT: ¿Qué vas a comprar para tu mamá?
SECOND STUDENT: Voy a comprar un suéter para mi mamá.

FIRST STUDENT: ¿Qué vas a comprar para tu papá?
SECOND STUDENT: Voy a comprar pantalones para mi papá.

FIRST STUDENT:	¿Qué vas a comprar para…(name)?
SECOND STUDENT:	Voy a comprar…para (name).
FIRST STUDENT:	¿Vas a comprar un banco?
SECOND STUDENT:	¡Eso es ridículo! No voy a comprar un banco.
FIRST STUDENT:	¿Vas a comprar un avión?
SECOND STUDENT:	No, ¡eso es ridículo! No voy a comprar un avión.

10.7 ORAL EXERCISE

Form groups of two students. One student will ask a question in Spanish from the list on the left, adding a word from the list on the right. The other student answers it.

	un suéter
	una blusa
	pantalones
	un autobús
	carne
	un tren
¿Va a comprar…?	tomates
Are you going to buy…?	gasolina
	pan
¿Vas a comprar…?	una bicicleta
Are you going to buy (fam.)…?	una motocicleta
	un avión
Voy a comprar…	un radio
I'm going to buy…	un disco compacto
	un televisor
No, no voy a comprar…	jamón
No, I'm not going to buy…	queso
	zapatos
No. ¡Eso es ridículo! No voy a comprar…	guantes
No. That's ridiculous! I'm not going to buy…	un vestido
	un león
	un sombrero
	chicle
	una camisa
	una antena parabólica

10.8 CONVERSATION VOCABULARY (OPTIONAL)

¡Ah, bueno!	*Oh, good!*	Hay muchos.	*There are many.*
¿Voy contigo?	*Shall I go with you?*	Hay muchas	*There are many things.*
Me gustaría…	*I would like…*	cosas.	
¿De qué color?	*What color?*	¿Vamos en	*Shall we go by bus?*
el traje	*suit (man's or*	autobús?	
	woman's)	parar	*to stop*
el abrigo	*coat*	¡Qué	*How convenient!*
Voy de compras.	*I'm going shopping.*	conveniente!	

🔊 10.9 CONVERSATION (OPTIONAL)

Form groups of two students each and conduct a conversation about shopping. The following block will serve as a guide for your conversation. However, do not restrict yourself only to what is in the block.

Shopping on Saturday morning

FIRST STUDENT:	¿Adónde vas esta mañana?
SECOND STUDENT:	Voy al centro. Voy de compras.
FIRST STUDENT:	¿Qué vas a comprar?
SECOND STUDENT:	Necesito un traje (vestido) para la fiesta.
FIRST STUDENT:	¡Ah, bueno! ¿Voy contigo?
SECOND STUDENT:	Sí, ven. Me gustaría.
FIRST STUDENT:	¿Vas a comprar un abrigo negro?
SECOND STUDENT:	No, azul. ¿Qué vas a comprar tú?
FIRST STUDENT:	Voy a comprar una blusa (camisa).
SECOND STUDENT:	¿De qué color?
FIRST STUDENT:	Necesito una blusa (camisa) blanca.
SECOND STUDENT:	También me gustaría comprar un suéter verde.
FIRST STUDENT:	En la tienda hay muchos.
SECOND STUDENT:	Sí, y hay muchos vestidos y trajes lindos también. Hay muchas cosas lindas.
FIRST STUDENT:	¿Vamos en autobús?
SECOND STUDENT:	Sí, el autobús para enfrente de la tienda.
FIRST STUDENT:	¡Qué conveniente!
SECOND STUDENT:	Sí, muy conveniente.
FIRST STUDENT:	Allí está el autobús.
SECOND STUDENT:	¡Vamos!

10.10 READING EXERCISE: EN LA TIENDA LA MODA

You are going to read an ad for the clothing store La Moda. Look at the ad, then answer the questions that follow.

TIENDA LA MODA

¡Tenemos toda la ropa que usted y su familia necesitan!
Y a los precios más bajos de la ciudad...

Mire estas ofertas increíbles:

PARA LAS DAMAS

faldas: de 20 a 30 euros

vestidos: de 40 a 50 euros

zapatos: de 30 a 35 euros

abrigos: de 80 a 85 euros

PARA LOS CABALLEROS

corbatas: todas a un sólo precio de 10 euros

suéteres: de 25 a 30 euros

zapatos: de 30 a 35 euros

trajes: de 75 a 80 euros

¡No se pierda usted estas gangas!

First see if you can match the following words from the ad:

1. precios
2. más bajos
3. ofertas
4. gangas

a. *offers*
b. *prices*
c. *lowest*
d. *bargains*

Now complete the following table, based on the information to the ad. (A euro is the currency of the European Economic Community, that is roughly equivalent to one U.S. dollar.) Write the names in Spanish of the items you can buy for the number of euros indicated in the correct columns.

10–20	20–30	30–40	40–50	50–60	60–70	70–80	80–90

10.11 WRITING EXERCISE

Look again at the ad for the La Moda clothing store. Imagine you have 200 euros to spend. What will you buy? What will you decide not to buy? Write at least six complete sentences describing your purchases.

VOCABULARY

NOUNS

la antena parabólica	*satellite dish*	el jamón	*ham*
		el libro	*book*
la bicicleta	*bicycle*	el regalo	*present, gift*
la camisa	*shirt*	el suéter	*sweater*
la casete, la cinta	*cassette, tape*	el televisor	*television set*
		la tienda de ropa	*the clothing store*
la corbata	*necktie*	el vestido	*dress*
el chicle	*gum*	los zapatos	*shoes*
la falda	*skirt*		

VERBS

depositar	*to deposit*

OTHER WORDS AND EXPRESSIONS

¿Adónde vas?	*Where are you going?*
¿En qué puedo servirle?	*How may I help you?*
¿Es todo?	*Is that all?*
ir + a + infinitive	*to be going to (infinitive)*
para	*for*
¿Qué?	*What?*
¿Qué vas a comprar?	*What are you going to buy?*
Quisiera…	*I would like…*
Necesito…	*I need…*
¿Va a comprar…?	*Are you going to buy…?*
¿Va a estar…?	*Are you going to be…?*
(No) Voy a comprar…	*I'm (not) going to buy…*

OPTIONAL LIST

NOUNS

el abrigo	coat
el traje	suit (man's or woman's)

OTHER WORDS AND EXPRESSIONS

¡Ah, bueno!	*Oh, good!*
¿De qué color?	*What color?*
Hay muchas.	*There are many things.*
Hay muchos. cosas.	*There are many.*
Me gustaría…	*I would like…*
parar	*to stop*
¡Qué conveniente!	*How convenient!*
¿Vamos en autobús?	*Shall we go by bus?*
¿Voy contigo?	*Shall I go with you?*
Voy de compras.	*I'm going shopping.*

LESSON 11

�֍

¡Vamos a leer!
- **-er** and **-ir** infinitives
- Expressing the future with **ir** + **a** + infinitive (continued)
- Using estar to express conditions
- Telling time

Grammar: **-er** and **-ir** infinitives

Not all infinitives (the **to** form) end in -**ar**. Some end in -**er** or -**ir**.

EXAMPLES:

vender	*to sell*	decidir	*to decide*
comprender	*to understand*	escribir	*to write*
comer	*to eat*	dormir	*to sleep*

11.1 LISTENING EXERCISE

Repeat each sentence after your instructor says it, reading along in the book as you speak.

1. **Voy a decidir.**
   I'm going to decide.

2. **Voy a dormir.**
   I'm going to sleep.

3. **Voy a vender la casa.**
   I'm going to sell the house.

4. **Voy a comer.**
   I'm going to eat.

5. **¿Va a decidir?**
   Are you going to decide?

6. **¿Va a dormir?**
   Are you going to sleep?

7. **¿Va a vender la casa?**
   Are you going to sell the house?

8. **¿Va a comer?**
   Are you going to eat?

11.2 LET'S READ!

el amigo	*the male friend*	¿Por qué?	*Why?*
la amiga	*the female friend*	¿Por qué	*Why don't you go…?*
el poema	*poem*	no va…?	
la novela	*novel*	Voy a vender	*I'm going to sell my*
la lección	*lesson*	mi bicicleta.	*bike.*
la carta	*letter*	Voy a escribir	*I'm going to write*
con	*with*	una carta.	*a letter.*
la frase	*sentence*	Voy a leer	*I'm going to read*
sus amigos	*your, his, her,*	un libro.	*a book.*
	their friends	Voy a salir	*I'm going out on*
la farmacia	*pharmacy*	el sábado.	*Saturday.*
la iglesia	*church*	Voy a estar	*I'm going to be at*
el reloj	*clock, watch*	en casa.	*home.*

📼 11.3 LISTENING EXERCISE

Repeat each sentence after your instructor says it, reading along in the book as you speak.

1. Voy a leer un libro interesante.
2. Voy a leer la lección.
3. Voy a escribir una carta
4. Voy a dormir el sábado.
5. Voy a escribir las frases.
6. No voy a vender la bicicleta.
7. No voy a vender el auto.
8. No voy a vender la casa.
9. No voy a estar en casa el sábado.
10. No voy a salir esta noche.

11.4 ORAL EXERCISE

Answer the following questions.

1. ¿Va a vender su bicicleta?
2. ¿Va a vender su libro de clase?
3. ¿Va a vender su estéreo?
4. ¿Va a vender su reloj?
5. ¿Va a escribir una carta?
6. ¿Va a escribir una carta en la clase?
7. ¿Va a escribir un libro?
8. ¿Va a escribir frases en la clase?
9. ¿Va a escribir un poema?
10. ¿Va a escribir una novela?
11. ¿Va a leer una novela?
12. ¿Va a leer una novela en la clase de español?
13. ¿Va a leer la lección esta noche?
14. ¿Va a dormir mucho esta noche?
15. ¿Va a dormir mucho este sábado?
16. ¿Va a estudiar la lección?
17. ¿Va a estar en casa esta noche?
18. ¿Va a estar en casa el sábado?

Can you do this exercise with your book closed?

Note: Notice that all the questions above use **Va**. In all the answers, you should use **Voy**.

11.5 ORAL OR WRITTEN EXERCISE

Change each of the following statements from the **yo** form (first person singular) into the **nosotros** form (first person plural).

EXAMPLE: **Voy a leer la lección.**
ANSWER: **Vamos a leer la lección.**

1. Voy a escribir las frases.
2. Voy a vender la bicicleta.
3. Voy a leer la novela.
4. Voy a estar en casa el sábado.
5. Voy al cine esta noche.
6. Voy a la fiesta.
7. Voy a trabajar mañana.
8. Voy a nadar mañana.
9. No voy a vender el auto.
10. Voy a comprar una bicicleta.

Grammar: Review of **ir** + **a** + infinitive

ir *to go*			
I go, I'm going	voy	vamos	*we go, we're going*
you go, you're going (fam.)	vas	vais	*you go, you're going (pl. fam.)*
you go, you're going (formal)		van	*you go, you're going (pl. formal)*
he goes, he's going			*they go, they're going*
she goes, she's going	va		
it goes, it's going			

Remember, you can express the future with every verb in the Spanish language (regular and irregular) by using a form of **ir** (from the chart above), plus **a**, plus the infinitive of any verb (regular or irregular).

EXAMPLES: Regular verbs

Voy a estudiar.   *I'm going to study.*

Alberto va a escribir   *Alberto is going to write*
  una carta.   *a letter.*

Vamos a cantar.   *We're going to sing.*

Van a leer.   *They are going to read.*

Irregular verbs

Voy a estar en casa.   *I'm going to be at home.*

Alberto va a   *Alberto is going to leave*
  salir mañana.   *tomorrow.*

Vamos a traer   *We're going to bring*
  el paquete.   *the package.*

Van a hacer   *They are going to make*
  limonada.   *lemonade.*

11.6 ORAL OR WRITTEN EXERCISE

Answer the following questions.

1. ¿Van usted y sus amigos al cine esta noche?

2. ¿Va a escribir frases en la clase de español?

3. ¿Va a hablar español en la clase de español?

4. ¿Va a escribir una carta esta noche?

5. ¿Va a estudiar mucho?

6. ¿Va a comprar un auto su mamá?

7. ¿Van a la fiesta mañana sus amigos?

8. ¿Van a escribir un poema usted y su papá?

9. ¿Van a ir al parque esta tarde sus amigos?

10. ¿Van a escribir un libro usted y su mamá?

11. ¿Va a comprar una bicicleta?

12. ¿Va a estar en casa el sábado?

13. ¿Va a escribir una carta en la clase?

14. ¿Va a leer un libro interesante?

Grammar: Using **estar** for conditions

The verb **estar** can also be used to express mental or physical conditions such as busyness, happiness, tiredness, sickness, readiness, etc.

EXAMPLES: **Estoy ocupado.**   *I'm busy.*
           Estamos cansados.   *We're tired.*

 ## 11.7 EVERYDAY EXPRESSIONS

Está ocupado.	*He is busy.*	**Está lista.**	*She is ready.*
Está contento.	*He is happy.*	**Estoy ocupada.**	*I'm busy. (fem.)*
Está cansado.	*He is tired.*	**Estoy cansada.**	*I'm tired. (fem.)*
Está enfermo.	*He is sick.*	**Estoy contenta.**	*I'm happy. (fem.)*
Está listo.	*He is ready.*	**¿Está listo?**	*Are you ready? (When you ask a man.)*
Estoy ocupado.	*I'm busy. (masc.)*		
Estoy cansado.	*I'm tired. (masc.)*	**¿Está lista?**	*Are you ready? (When you ask a woman.)*
Estoy contento.	*I'm happy. (masc.)*		
Está ocupada.	*She is busy.*	**¿Están listos?**	*Are you ready? (When you ask men and women or boys and girls.)*
Está contenta.	*She is happy.*		
Está cansada.	*She is tired.*		
Está enferma.	*She is sick.*		

11.8 ORAL OR WRITTEN EXERCISE

Combine words from the three columns below to form complete sentences. Create sentences that express your plan and your friends' plans.

Voy…	al parque	mañana
Vamos…	al cine	con (nombre)
¿Por qué no va…?	a la fiesta	esta noche
Va…	a la clase	esta tarde
Van…	al restaurante	esta mañana
	al supermercado	el sábado
	a la tienda	el lunes
	a la farmacia	el viernes

11.9 CONVERSATION VOCABULARY

a la una	*at one o'clock*	a las siete	*at seven o'clock*
a las dos	*at two o'clock*	a las ocho	*at eight o'clock*
a las tres	*at three o'clock*	a las nueve	*at nine o'clock*
a las cuatro	*at four o'clock*	a las diez	*at ten o'clock*
a las cinco	*at five o'clock*	a las once	*at eleven o'clock*
a las seis	*at six o'clock*	a las doce	*at twelve o'clock*

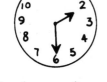

a las dos y media *at two-thirty (at two and a half)*   **a las tres y media** *at three-thirty (at three and a half)*   **a las cinco y media** *at five-thirty (at five and a half)*

a las tres y cuarto *at a quarter past three (at three and a quarter)*   **a las diez y cuarto** *at a quarter past ten (at ten and a quarter)*   **a las cuatro menos cuarto** *at a quarter before four (at four minus a quarter)*

¿A qué hora?	*At what time? (At what hour?)*	¿Qué hora es?	*What time is it?*
¿Cuándo?	*When?*	Es la una.	*It's one o'clock.*
una hora	*one hour*	Son las dos.	*It's two o'clock.*
en una hora	*in an hour*	Son las tres	*It's three o'clock*
en cinco minutos	*in five minutes*	(cuatro, etc.)	*(four o'clock, etc.)*
		de la mañana	*in the morning*
en diez minutos	*in ten minutes*	de la tarde	*in the afternoon*
en media hora	*in half an hour*	de la noche	*in the night (at night)*
en una semana	*in a week*	¿Cuándo va	*When are you going*
en un mes	*in a month*	a terminar?	*to finish?*
en un año	*in a year*	¿A qué	*At what time are*
más tarde	*later*	hora va?	*you going?*

Note: You will learn how to give more precise times in Lesson 15.

11.10 CONVERSATION

Your instructor will point to two students who will ask each other where they are going. Take turns asking and answering the questions. Use your imagination. Combine the sentences in different ways. Invent questions and answers.

The following block will serve as a guide for your conversation. However, do not restrict yourself only to what is in the block.

At what time?

FIRST STUDENT: ¿A qué hora vas al concierto?
SECOND STUDENT: A las siete y media.
FIRST STUDENT: ¿A qué hora vas al restaurante?
SECOND STUDENT: A las doce.
FIRST STUDENT: ¿A qué hora vas a la estación?
SECOND STUDENT: A las tres.
FIRST STUDENT: ¿A qué hora vas al despacho?
SECOND STUDENT: A las nueve.
FIRST STUDENT: ¿A qué hora vas a la iglesia?
SECOND STUDENT: A las once.
FIRST STUDENT: ¿Cuándo vas a la clase?

SECOND STUDENT: En cinco minutos.
 FIRST STUDENT: ¿Cuándo vas al cine?
SECOND STUDENT: En diez minutos.
 FIRST STUDENT: ¿Cuándo vas al fútbol?
SECOND STUDENT: En una hora.
 FIRST STUDENT: ¿Cuándo va a Washington?
SECOND STUDENT: En una semana.
 FIRST STUDENT: ¿Cuándo va a terminar?
SECOND STUDENT: En cinco minutos.

11.11 CONVERSATION VOCABULARY (OPTIONAL)

¿Vas al fútbol?	*Are you going to the soccer game?*
Pedro viene este fin de semana.	*Pedro is coming this weekend.*
¿Dónde vive Pedro?	*Where does Pedro live?*
Allí viene Pedro.	*Here comes Pedro.*
¿Quién es Pedro?	*Who is Pedro?*
Es un amigo.	*He's a friend.*
¿Viene en avión?	*Is he coming by plane?*
recibir	*to meet (to receive)*
a recibirlo	*to meet him (to receive him)*
simpático(a)	*nice*
Escribe comedias para la televisión.	*He writes television comedies.*

11.12 CONVERSATION (OPTIONAL)

Form groups of three students each and conduct a conversation. The following block will serve as a guide for your conversation. However, do not restrict yourself only to what is in the block.

Pedro comes to visit.

FIRST STUDENT:	¿Vas al fútbol?
SECOND STUDENT:	No. Pedro viene el sábado.
FIRST STUDENT:	¿Dónde vive Pedro?
SECOND STUDENT:	Vive en San Antonio.
FIRST STUDENT:	Mira. Allí viene (name of third student).
SECOND STUDENT:	(Calling third student) (¡Name!) Ven acá.
THIRD STUDENT:	Buenas tardes.
FIRST AND SECOND STUDENTS:	Buenas tardes.
THIRD STUDENT:	¿Van al fútbol el sábado?
SECOND STUDENT:	No. Pedro viene el sábado.
THIRD STUDENT:	¿Quién es Pedro?
FIRST STUDENT:	Es un amigo. Es de San Antonio.
THIRD STUDENT:	¿Viene en avión?
SECOND STUDENT:	Sí. Vamos al aeropuerto a recibirlo.
FIRST STUDENT:	Pedro es muy simpático.
SECOND STUDENT:	Sí, muy simpático.
FIRST STUDENT:	¿Dónde trabaja?
SECOND STUDENT:	Trabaja en una estación de televisión.
THIRD STUDENT:	¿Es actor?
SECOND STUDENT:	No. Escribe comedias para la televisión.
THIRD STUDENT:	¿Escribe bien?
SECOND STUDENT:	Sí, muy bien. Escribe comedias excelentes.

Grammar: Meanings of the verb ir

Remember how to form the verb **ir** in the present tense. Later on, we will learn other uses of **ir**. Here are all the meanings of the verb **ir** in the present tense for you to review.

	STATEMENTS		QUESTIONS
Voy.	*I go. I'm going.*	**¿Voy?**	*Do I go? Am I going?*
Vas.	*You go. You are going. (fam.)*	**¿Vas?**	*Do you go? Are you going?*
Va.	*You go. You are going.*		
	He goes. He is going.	**¿Va?**	*Do you go? Are you going?*
	She goes. She is going.		*Does he go? Is he going?*
	It goes. It is going.		*Does she go? Is she going?*
Vamos.	*We go. We are going.*		*Does it go? Is it going?*
Van.	*You go. You are going. (pl.)*	**¿Vamos?**	*Do we go? Are we going?*
	They go. They are going.	**¿Van?**	*Do you go? Are you going? (pl.)*
			Do they go? Are they going?

EXAMPLES:	**¿Va todos los días?**	*Do you go every day?*
	Va con frecuencia.	*You go/He/She/It goes frequently.*
	Nunca va.	*You go/He/She/It never goes.*

11.13 READING EXERCISE: LOS CONCIERTOS CLÁSICOS

In this lesson, you learned how to tell time. Look at the following partial listing of classical programs on **El Canal Clásico de Radiotelevisión Española**, then answer the questions that follow.

Notice that the programs are given as 24-hour listings. This is a European way to show time without telling A.M. or P.M. Any number larger than twelve is in the afternoon, any number lower than twelve is in the morning. To convert to P.M., subtract the number 12 from the time given.

EXAMPLES: 18:30 = 6:30 P.M.
18:45 = 9:45 P.M. ... 21:45 = 9:45 P.M.

08:00 A LAS OCHO CON LA O.S.R.T.V.E.
Dirección: James Loughram
Orquesta: Orquesta Sinfónica de RTVE
Desde el Teatro Monumental de Madrid, actuación de la Orquesta Sinfónica de RTVE que, bajo la dirección de James Loughram, interpreta "Variaciones Enigma" de Edward Elgar.

10:05 CÓMO SE HIZO "SEVILLANAS"
Dirección: Carlos Saura
Cómo se realizó la película "Sevillanas." Documental — musical — color

11:45 MOSAICO BARROCO
Intérpretes: Brandenbug Consort, Rachel Brown, Sally Jackson, Roy Goodman
Dirección de orquesta: Roy Goodman
Piezas cortas de Doménico Gallo, Georg Friedrich Handel, Henry Purcell, Johann Joseph Fux, Johann Pachelbel y Matthew Locke.

15:50 CON FIRMA. MONOGRÁFICOS
Homenaje a Jacinto Guerrero
Dirección: Mario Moreno, Enrique García Asensio
Desde el Teatro Monumental de Madrid, actuación de la Orquesta Sinfónica y Coro de RTVE que, bajo la direc-

ción de Enrique García Asensio, interpreta de la obra "La Alsaciana" de Jacinto Guerrero.

20:00 A LAS OCHO CON LA O.S.R.T.V.E.
Dirección: Vernon Handley
Orquesta: Orquesta Sinfónica de RTVE
Desde el Teatro Monumental de Madrid, actuación de la Orquesta Sinfónica de RTVE que, bajo la dirección de Vernon Handley, interpreta la "Sinfonía Número 5 en Re Mayor" de Ralph Vaughan Williams.

23:50 LAS OTRAS DANZAS
Grupo Argia
Reportaje sobre el grupo de danza tradicional del País Vasco "Argia", cuyo director es Juan Antonio Urbeltz.

01:05 PURO Y JONDO
Nano de Jerez
Dirección: Manuel Ponce
"Puro y Jondo" es una serie dedicada al cante flamenco más tradicional, en la que intervienen artistas exclusivamente andaluces y, en su mayoría, de etnia gitana. "Tío Juane" fue uno de los más destacados herreros del barrio de Santiago en Jerez de la Frontera. Su hijo "Nano" de Jerez sigue la estela paterna del cante, con gran pureza y ajustado compás.

1. ¿A qué hora es el documental del famoso director español Carlos Saura?
2. ¿A qué hora es el programa sobre las danzas tradicionales del País Vasco?
3. ¿A qué hora es el concierto de la música de "Variaciones Enigma" de Edward Elgar?
4. ¿A qué hora es el concierto de la música de Purcell, Gallo, Handel y Pachelbel?
5. ¿A qué hora es el programa sobre la música flamenca?
6. ¿Qué programa es más interesante para usted?, ¿y menos interesante?

11.14 WRITING EXERCISE

What do you normally watch on television? Suppose you had a day free to watch as much or as little television as you would like. Write five to six sentences saying what you would watch (or what else you would do) at the times given.

9:00 A.M.

11:00 A.M.

4:00 P.M.

8:00 P.M.

9:00 P.M.

10:00 P.M.

VOCABULARY

NOUNS

la amiga	*the female friend*	la lección	*lesson*
el amigo	*the male friend*	la novela	*novel*
el año	*year*	la media hora	*half hour*
la carta	*letter*	el mes	*month*
la farmacia	*pharmacy*	el minuto	*minute*
la frase	*sentence*	el poema	*poem*
la hora	*hour*	el reloj	*clock, watch*
la iglesia	*church*		

VERBS

comer	*to eat*	escribir	*to write*
comprender	*to understand*	leer	*to read*
decidir	*to decide*	vender	*to sell*
dormir	*to sleep*		

ADJECTIVES

cansado(a)	*tired*	listo(a)	*ready*
contento(a)	*happy*	ocupado(a)	*busy*
enfermo(a)	*sick*		

OTHER WORDS AND EXPRESSIONS

a la una	*at one o'clock*	en cinco (diez) minutos	*in five (ten) minutes*
a las dos (tres, etc.)	*at two (three, etc.) o'clock*	en media hora	*in half an hour*
a las dos (tres, etc.) menos cuarto	*at a quarter before two (three, etc.)*	en una semana (mes, año)	*in a week (month, year)*
		estar + adjective	*to be (physical or mental condition)*
a las dos (tres, etc.) y cuarto	*at a quarter past two (three, etc.)*	estar en casa	*to be at home*
a las dos (tres, etc.) y media	*at two (three, etc.) thirty*	más tarde	*later*
		¿Por qué?	*Why?*
¿A qué hora?	*At what time?*	¿Por qué no va...?	*Why don't you go...?*
con	*with*	¿Qué hora es?	*What time is it?*
¿Cuándo?	*When?*	Es la una.	*It is one o'clock.*
¿Cuándo va a...?	*When are you going to...?*	Son las dos (tres, etc.)	*It is two (three, etc.) o'clock.*
Voy a...	*I'm going to...*	de la mañana (tarde, noche)	*in the morning (afternoon, evening)*

OPTIONAL LIST

VERBS

recibir	*to meet, to receive*

OTHER WORDS AND EXPRESSIONS

a recibirlo	*to meet him (to receive him)*	¿Dónde vive (name)?	*Where does (name) live?*
Allí viene (name).	*Here comes (name).*	Escribe comedias para la televisión.	*He writes television comedies.*
las comedias para la televisión	*television comedies*	¿Quién es (name)?	*Who is (name)?*
		simpático	*nice*

LESSON 12

✳

¿Lees el periódico?

- The present tense of **-er** and **-ir** verbs, singular forms
- Using **estar** to express conditions (continued)

Grammar: The present tense of **-er** and **-ir** verbs, singular forms

To form the singular present tense of -er and -ir verbs, remove the -er or -ir and add -**o** for the **yo** form, -**es** for the **tú** form, and -**e** for the usted and third person forms.

EXAMPLES:

vender *to sell*	
I sell, I'm selling	vendo
you sell, you're selling (fam.)	vendes
you sell, you're selling (formal)	
he sells, he's selling	vende
she sells, she's selling	

vivir *to live*	
I live, I'm living	vivo
you live, you're living (fam.)	vives
you live, you're living (formal)	
he lives, he's living	vive
she lives, she's living	

EXAMPLES: **Elena vende su auto.**   *Elena sells, is selling her car.*
Vivo en Buenos Aires. *I live, am living in Buenos Aires.*
¿Dónde vives?   *Where do you live?*

12.1 NEWSPAPER WRITING

solo	alone (masc.)	**Vivo...**	*I live...*
sola	alone (fem.)	**Escribo...**	*I write...*
mi familia	my family	**Vendo...**	*I sell...*
el periódico	newspaper	**Leo...**	*I read...*
el artículo	article	**Recibo...**	*I receive...*
el compañero de cuarto	the male roommate	**Comprendo.**	*I understand.*
		¿Vive usted...?	*Do you live...?*
la compañera de cuarto	the female roommate	**¿Escribe usted...?**	*Do you write...?*
		¿Vende usted...?	*Do you sell...?*
el periodista	journalist	**¿Lee usted...?**	*Do you read...?*
muy bien	very well	**¿Recibe usted...?**	*Do you receive...?*
la medicina	medicine	**¿Comprende usted?**	*Do you understand?*
el lápiz	pencil		

 ## 12.2 LISTENING EXERCISE

Repeat each sentence after your instructor says it, reading along in the book as you speak.

1. ¿Dónde vive Roberto?
2. Roberto vive en Venezuela.
3. Vivo con mi familia.
4. Escribo muchas cartas.
5. El periodista escribe artículos.
6. Leo el periódico.
7. María lee mucho.
8. Carlos vende medicinas.
9. Alberto no vende periódicos.
10. Recibo muchas cartas.
11. ¿Dónde vive usted?

Grammar: How to use the present tense of **-er** and **-ir** verbs

Very important: When you speak *about* any person other than yourself (singular), end the verb in -e.

EXAMPLES:

Alberto recibe muchas cartas.	*Alberto receives many letters.*
María comprende italiano.	*María understands Italian.*
Carlos vende autos.	*Carlos sells cars.*
Roberto vive en San Francisco.	*Roberto lives in San Francisco.*
¿Comprende?	*Do you understand?*

When you are talking directly *to* someone, the verb form ends in **-es** or **-e**, depending on how well you know the person.

EXAMPLES:

Tú escribes novelas.	*You write novels. (fam.)*
Tú vendes ropa.	*You sell clothing. (fam.)*
Usted comprende la lección.	*You understand the lesson. (polite)*

When you speak about yourself in the present tense, end all regular verbs in **-o**. This applies to **-ar**, **-er**, and **-ir** verbs.

EXAMPLES:

comprar	*to buy*	Compro...	*I buy...*
vender	*to sell*	Vendo...	*I sell...*
vivir	*to live*	Vivo...	*I live...*
escribir	*to write*	Escribo...	*I write...*

Remember to stress the next-to-the-last syllable of all verbs in the present tense, like this:

VI-vo	com-PREN-do
es-CRI-bo	tra-BA-jo

12.3 ORAL EXERCISE

Answer the following questions.

EXAMPLE: **¿Dónde vive Alberto?**
ANSWER: **Alberto vive en Colombia.**

1. ¿Dónde vive usted?

2. ¿Dónde vive su familia?

3. ¿Vive usted en una ciudad?

4. ¿Vive usted en una casa?

5. ¿Vive usted solo (sola)?

6. ¿Vive con un compañero de cuarto (una compañera de cuarto)?

7. ¿Estudia usted español?

8. ¿Estudia su compañero de cuarto (compañera de cuarto) español?

9. ¿Escribe usted en la clase?

10. ¿Escribe usted muchas cartas?

11. ¿Recibe usted muchas cartas?

12. ¿Escribe usted artículos para el periódico?

13. ¿Quién escribe artículos para el periódico?

14. ¿Lee usted el periódico?

15. ¿Comprende usted el periódico?

16. ¿Lee usted libros interesantes?

17. ¿Lee usted mucho?

18. ¿Lee mucho su compañero de cuarto (compañera de cuarto)?

19. ¿Dónde trabaja su papá?

20. ¿Dónde trabaja su mamá?

21. ¿Qué vende la farmacia?

22. ¿Vende usted libros?

23. ¿Vende usted periódicos?

24. ¿Comprende usted la lección?

Can you do this exercise with your book closed?

12.4 ORAL EXERCISE

Answer the following questions.

1. ¿Habla usted español?

2. ¿Lee mucho?

3. ¿Comprende usted el libro?

4. ¿Vive usted solo (sola)?

5. ¿Va al cine esta noche?

6. ¿Va a vender la bicicleta?

7. ¿Recibe usted muchas cartas?

8. ¿Va a leer el periódico?

9. ¿Escribe usted muchas cartas?

10. ¿Dónde está su paraguas?

11. ¿Estudia usted mucho?

12. ¿Comprende usted la lección?

13. ¿Dónde vive usted?

14. ¿Lee usted el periódico?

12.5 WRITTEN OR ORAL EXERCISE

Change the following verbs in the **yo** form into the **usted** and **tú** forms.

EXAMPLE: **vivo**
ANSWER: **vive, vives**

1. escribo
2. vendo
3. recibo
4. comprendo
5. leo

12.6 EVERYDAY EXPRESSIONS

Está solo.	*He's alone.*	**Sí, amigo.**	*Yes, my friend. (masc)*
Está sola.	*She's alone.*	**Sí, amiga.**	*Yes, my friend. (fem.)*
Está triste.	*He's sad. She's sad.*	**¡Caramba!**	*Gee whiz! Gosh! Darn!*
Está mejor.	*He's better. She's better.*	**media naranja**	*half an orange*
Está peor.	*He's worse. She's worse.*	**mi media naranja**	*my husband, my wife (my half orange, idiomatic use)*
Está bien.	*He's well. She's well. It's all right. It's O.K.*	**mi pareja**	*my partner, spouse*
		mi esposo(a)	*my husband, wife*
¿Está bien?	*Is he well? Is she well? Is it all right? Is it O.K?*		

12.7 COMPOSITION VOCABULARY

tomar	*to take*	el Viejo	*Old San Juan*
las tiendas	*different stores*	San Juan	
diferentes		después	*afterwards*
la música	*Puerto Rican music*	encontrar	*to meet*
puertorriqueña		Isla Verde	*Green Island*
porque	*because*	el Morro	*an old fortress in San Juan*
los restaurantes	*typical restaurants*	la universidad	*the university*
típicos		típico(a)	*typical*
con ellos	*with them*	cerca de	*near*

12.8 LISTENING EXERCISE

Listen to the following composition as your instructor reads it aloud.

Roberto va a Puerto Rico.

    Mi amigo Roberto va a San Juan, Puerto Rico, con su familia. Está muy contento porque va en avión. Va a tomar el avión en el aeropuerto. En San Juan, Roberto, su papá y mamá van a tomar un taxi y van a un hotel excelente que está en Isla Verde, cerca del centro de la ciudad. El hotel está en la playa, enfrente del mar. Roberto va a encontrar a unos amigos en la playa y va a hablar español con ellos.

    Roberto y su familia van a las tiendas en el Viejo San Juan, en el centro de la ciudad. Roberto va a comprar un sombrero puertorriqueño, una guitarra y muchos discos compactos. Después, van a visitar el Morro y la universidad. También van al cine, al teatro y a muchos restaurantes típicos.

12.9 ORAL EXERCISE (OPTIONAL)

Read each sentence in the previous composition and translate it into English.

12.10 ORAL OR WRITTEN MINI-TEST (OPTIONAL)

Answer these questions to show how well you understood the composition.

1. ¿Adónde va Roberto?
2. ¿Va en tren?
3. ¿Dónde está el hotel de Roberto?
4. ¿Va a hablar Roberto con sus amigos?
5. ¿Va a comprar una guitarra?
6. ¿Va a comprar discos compactos?
7. ¿Está triste Roberto?
8. ¿Está en la playa el hotel?
9. ¿Va a las tiendas Roberto?
10. ¿Va al museo Roberto?
11. ¿Va a muchos restaurantes?
12. ¿Va a visitar la universidad?

Grammar: The irregular verb **salir**

Remember: Verbs that do not follow the rules for regular verbs are called irregular verbs. Here is an irregular verb: **salir** (*to go out*).

If this verb were regular, the first person singular would be "salo". Instead, you insert a **g** and it become **salgo**. This is what makes **salir** irregular.

salir *to go*	
I go out, I leave (a place)	**salgo**
you go out, you leave (fam.)	**sales**
you go out, you leave (formal) *he goes out, he leaves* *she goes out, she leaves*	**sale**

EXAMPLES: —¿**Sales a las tres?**   *Are you leaving at three?*
—**No, salgo temprano,**   *No, I'm leaving early, at two-thirty.*
a las dos y media.

Notice that only the **yo** form is irregular. The rest of the singular forms follow the rules for regular -**er** and -**ir** verbs.

12.11 LISTENING EXERCISE

Repeat each sentence after your instructor says it, reading along in the book as you speak.

1. ¿A qué hora sale el tren?
2. ¿A qué hora sale el avión?
3. ¿A qué hora sale el autobús?
4. El autobús sale a las tres.
5. ¿A qué hora sale Alberto?
6. ¿A qué hora sale su papá?
7. ¿A qué hora sale su mamá?
8. ¿A qué hora sale usted?
9. ¿A qué hora sales tú?
10. Sale a tiempo.

12.12 CONVERSATION VOCABULARY (OPTIONAL)

generalmente	*generally*	**Sale tarde.**	*He/She/It leaves late.*
el doctor	*the male doctor*	**Es muy tarde.**	*It's very late.*
la doctora	*the female doctor*	**Es muy temprano.**	*It's very early.*
¿A qué hora sale del trabajo?	*At what time do you leave work?*	**a tiempo**	*on time*
		Sale a tiempo.	*He/She/It leaves on time.*
¿A qué hora sale de la clase?	*At what time do you leave the class?*	**tu**	*your (fam.)*
		mi mejor amigo	*my best friend*
tarde	*late*	**mi tío**	*my uncle*
temprano	*early*	**mi tía**	*my aunt*

12.13 CONVERSATION (OPTIONAL)

One student will ask a question and another student will answer it. Take turns asking and answering the questions, based on the chart provided. After you have asked three questions, give other students a chance to do the same. Ask any questions you want, provided you ask them in Spanish.

The following block will serve as a guide for your conversation. However, do not restrict yourself only to what is in the block.

At what time do you leave? At what time does he (she, it) leave?

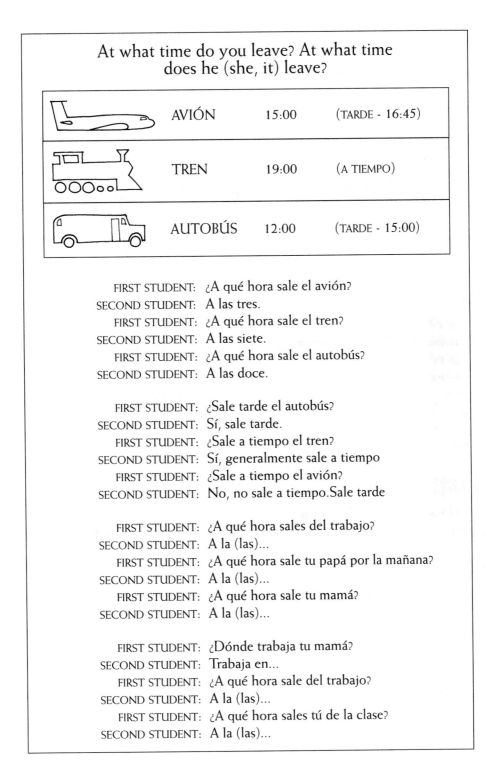

	AVIÓN	15:00	(TARDE - 16:45)
	TREN	19:00	(A TIEMPO)
	AUTOBÚS	12:00	(TARDE - 15:00)

FIRST STUDENT: ¿A qué hora sale el avión?
SECOND STUDENT: A las tres.
FIRST STUDENT: ¿A qué hora sale el tren?
SECOND STUDENT: A las siete.
FIRST STUDENT: ¿A qué hora sale el autobús?
SECOND STUDENT: A las doce.

FIRST STUDENT: ¿Sale tarde el autobús?
SECOND STUDENT: Sí, sale tarde.
FIRST STUDENT: ¿Sale a tiempo el tren?
SECOND STUDENT: Sí, generalmente sale a tiempo
FIRST STUDENT: ¿Sale a tiempo el avión?
SECOND STUDENT: No, no sale a tiempo.Sale tarde

FIRST STUDENT: ¿A qué hora sales del trabajo?
SECOND STUDENT: A la (las)...
FIRST STUDENT: ¿A qué hora sale tu papá por la mañana?
SECOND STUDENT: A la (las)...
FIRST STUDENT: ¿A qué hora sale tu mamá?
SECOND STUDENT: A la (las)...

FIRST STUDENT: ¿Dónde trabaja tu mamá?
SECOND STUDENT: Trabaja en...
FIRST STUDENT: ¿A qué hora sale del trabajo?
SECOND STUDENT: A la (las)...
FIRST STUDENT: ¿A qué hora sales tú de la clase?
SECOND STUDENT: A la (las)...

FIRST STUDENT:	¿Dónde trabaja tu tío?
SECOND STUDENT:	Trabaja en...
FIRST STUDENT:	¿A qué hora sale del trabajo?
SECOND STUDENT:	A la (las)...
FIRST STUDENT:	¡Caramba! Sale muy tarde (temprano)
SECOND STUDENT:	Sí, muy tarde (temprano).

12.14 ORAL OR WRITTEN EXERCISE (OPTIONAL)

Form complete sentences by combining the words in the three columns. Create your own sentences. Use any names or times you want.

El tren		tarde
El avión		a tiempo
El autobús		muy tarde
El doctor		a la una
La doctora	salgo	a las dos
Mi tío	sales	a las tres
Mi tía	sale	a las cinco
Mi amigo mejor		a las tres y media
Mi amiga mejor		a las cinco y media
Yo		a las dos y media
Tú		a las cuatro y cuarenta
		a las...
		temprano

12.15 READING EXERCISE: UNA CARTA A TÍA ELENA

In this lesson, you learned to talk about how you and others are feeling, and to discuss the things you read, such as the newspaper. Read the following letter to a newspaper advice columnist, Tía Elena. Then answer the questions that follow.

Querida Tía Elena:

Le escribo esta carta porque estoy muy triste. Estoy solo todo el día porque mi esposa trabaja y yo no tengo trabajo. Ella trabaja en una oficina y a veces trabaja hasta 60 o 70 horas a la semana. Sale de la casa muy temprano, a las cinco, y no regresa a casa hasta las nueve o diez de la noche. Me gusta pasar tiempo con ella, pero no es posible, a causa de sus horas de trabajo. Estoy muy melancólico y a veces muy nervioso. ¿Comprende Ud. mi problema?

Un esposo solitario

Querido Esposo Solitario:

Sí, comprendo su problema. Ya es hora de hablar francamente con su pareja. Ustedes necesitan encontrar un equilibrio. Usted necesita buscar trabajo inmediatamente y su esposa necesita trabajar menos. Si no es posible, deben buscar algún tipo de compromiso. Ustedes tiene dos rutinas muy diferentes y es difícil pasar tiempo juntos. ¡Buena suerte! Estoy segura de que encontrarán una solución.

Tía Elena

Match the phrases on the left with their meanings on the right.

1. **porque** estoy muy triste

2. me gusta **pasar tiempo**

3. hablar **francamente**

4. **encontrar** un equilibrio

5. **buscar** trabajo inmediatamente

6. trabajar **menos**

7. **deben** buscar algún tipo de compromiso

8. **¡Buena suerte!**

9. Estoy **segura de que encontrarán**

a. to speak frankly

b. because I'm very sad

c. Good luck!

d. I'm sure that you will find

e. I like to spend time

f. to find an equilibrium

g. to look for work immediately

h. to work less

i. you should look for some kind of compromise

Now answer the following questions.

1. ¿Cómo está Esposo Solitario?

2. ¿Cuándo sale la esposa de la casa? ¿Cuándo regresa?

3. ¿Trabaja Esposo Solitario?

4. ¿Comprende Tía Elena el problema?

5. ¿Qué necesita buscar Esposo Solitario?

6. ¿Qué necesita hacer la esposa?

12.16 WRITING EXERCISE

What do you read and write during a typical week? Write five to six sentences that say what you write and read and what days of the week you normally do each.

VOCABULARY

NOUNS

el artículo	*article*	el lápiz	*pencil*
el compañero de cuarto	*the male roommate*	la medicina	*medicine*
		la música	*music*
la compañera de cuarto	*the female roommate*	el periódico	*newspaper*
		el periodista	*journalist*
la familia	*family*	la universidad	*university*

VERBS

encontrar	*to meet*	tomar	*to take*
salir	*to leave*	vivir	*to live*

ADJECTIVES

bien	*well (masc. fem.)*	puertorriqueño(a)	*Puerto Rican (masc. fem.)*
diferente	*different (masc. fem.)*	solo(a)	*alone (masc. fem.)*
mejor	*better (masc. fem.)*	típico(a)	*typical (masc. fem.)*
peor	*worse (masc. fem.)*	triste	*sad (masc. fem.)*

OTHER WORDS AND EXPRESSIONS

¡Caramba!	*Gee whiz! Gosh! Darn!*	mi media naranja	*my husband, my wife, my partner (idiomatic)*
después	*afterwards*		
Cerca de con ellos	*near with them*	mi pareja	*my partner, spouse*
		muy bien	*very well*
¿Está bien?	*Is he (she) well? Is it all right? Is it O.K.?*	porque	*because*
		media naranja	*half an orange.*
		Sí, amigo(a).	*Yes, my friend.*
mi esposo(a)	*my husband, wife*		

OPTIONAL LIST

NOUNS

el doctor	*the male doctor*	**el tío**	*the uncle*
la doctora	*the female doctor*	**la tía**	*the aunt*

ADJECTIVES

tarde	*late*
temprano	*early*

OTHER WORDS AND EXPRESSIONS

¿A qué hora sale de...?	At what time do you leave...?	**Es muy tarde (temprano).**	*It's very late (early).*
a tiempo	*on time*	**generalmente**	*generally*
el mejor amigo	*the best friend (male)*	**tu**	*your (fam.)*
la mejor amiga	*the best friend (female)*		

LESSON 13

✳

¿Qué venden?

- The present tense of all regular **-er** and **-ir** verbs
- Talking about stores and the merchandise they sell

Grammar: Forming the present tense endings of all regular -er and -ir verbs

To form the present tense of all regular -er and -ir verbs, remove the -er or -ir and add the following endings.

Present tense endings of -er verbs

I	-o	-emos	we
you (fam.)	-es	-éis	you (pl. fam.)
you (formal)			you (pl. formal)
he	-e	-en	they
she			

Present tense endings of -ir verbs

I	-o	-imos	we
you (fam.)	-es	-is	you (pl. fam.)
you (formal)			you (pl. formal)
he	-e	-en	them
she			

vender *to sell*

I sell, I'm selling	vendo	vendemos	we sell, we're selling
you sell, you're selling (fam.)	vendes	vendéis	you sell, you're selling (pl. fam.)
you sell, you're selling (formal)		venden	you sell, you're selling (pl. formal)
he sells, she's selling	vende		they sell, they're selling
she sells, she's selling			

vivir *to live*		
I live, I'm living	**vivo**	**vivimos**	*we live, we're living*
you live, you're living (fam.)	**vives**	**vivís**	*you live, you're living (pl. fam.)*
you live, you're living (formal)			*you live, you're living (pl. formal)*
he lives, he's living	**vive**	**viven**	*they live, they're living*
she lives, she's living			

EXAMPLES: **Los Ruiz viven en Santa Fe.**   *The Ruiz family lives in Santa Fe.*
Venden autos.   *They sell cars.*
¿Dónde vives tú?   *Where do you live?*

13.1 LISTENING EXERCISE

Repeat each word after your instructor says it, reading along in the book as you speak. Remember to stress the next-to-last syllable of each verb in the present tense.

1. vendo
2. vendes
3. vende
4. vendemos
5. venden

6. vivo
7. vives
8. vive
9. vivimos
10. viven

13.2 AT SCHOOL

la persona	*person*	**Escribimos.**	*We write.*
Comprendemos.	*We understand.*	**¿Escribimos?**	*Do we write?*
¿Comprendemos?	*Do we understand?*	**Escriben.**	*They write.*
Comprenden.	*They understand.*	**¿Escriben?**	*Do they write?*
¿Comprenden?	*Do they understand?*	**Vivimos...**	*We live...*
Leemos.	*We read.*	**¿Vivimos...?**	*Do we live...?*
¿Leemos?	*Do we read?*	**Viven...**	*They live...*
Leen.	*They read.*	**¿Viven...?**	*Do they live...?*
¿Leen?	*Do they read?*		

13.3 LISTENING EXERCISE

Repeat each sentence after your instructor says it, reading along in the book as you speak.

1. ¿Escriben artículos los estudiantes?
2. ¿Escriben novelas los estudiantes?
3. Los italianos viven en Italia.
4. Los chilenos viven en Chile.
5. Leemos el libro en la clase.
6. No leemos novelas en la clase.
7. No leemos el periódico en la clase.
8. Escribimos muchas frases en la clase.
9. Los periodistas escriben artículos.
10. Los estudiantes comprenden la lección.

13.4 ORAL EXERCISE

Answer the following questions.

1. ¿Dónde viven los italianos?
2. ¿Dónde viven los chilenos?
3. ¿Dónde viven los mexicanos?
4. ¿Leemos muchas frases en la clase?
5. ¿Leemos novelas en la clase?
6. ¿Leemos el libro en la clase?
7. ¿Leen mucho tu tío y tu tía?
8. ¿Comprende usted la lección?

9. ¿Escribe usted frases?

10. ¿Escribe usted muchas frases en la clase?

11. ¿Escribimos cartas en la clase?

12. ¿Escribimos artículos en la clase?

13. ¿Escriben artículos los periodistas?

14. ¿Leemos el periódico en la clase?

15. ¿Dónde vive usted en la universidad?

16. ¿Dónde vive su familia?

17. ¿Dónde vive su mejor amigo?

18. ¿Dónde viven sus amigos en la universidad?

Can you do this exercise with your book closed?

13.5 ORAL OR WRITTEN EXERCISE

Change the following verbs from the infinitive into the third person plural form.

EXAMPLE: **venden**
ANSWER: **venden**

1. comprender	4. leer	7. comprar
2. vivir	5. recibir	8. nadar
3. escribir	6. hablar	9. trabajar

13.6 ORAL OR WRITTEN EXERCISE

Answer the following questions.

EXAMPLE: **¿Escribimos artículos en la clase?**
ANSWER: **No, no escribimos artículos en la clase.**

1. ¿Escribimos poemas en la clase?

2. ¿Escribimos novelas en la clase?

3. ¿Escribimos frases en la clase?

4. ¿Leemos libros en la clase?

5. ¿Comprendemos la lección?

6. ¿Lee usted el periódico en la clase?

7. ¿Dónde lee usted el periódico?

8. ¿Lee usted muchas novelas?

9. ¿Leen usted y sus amigos muchos poemas?

10. ¿Nada usted mucho?

11. ¿Estudian mucho usted y sus amigos?

12. ¿Escribe usted muchas cartas?

13.7 CONVERSATION VOCABULARY

WORDS YOU KNOW

la fruta	*fruit*	**la fresa**	*strawberry*
la pera	*pear*	**la blusa**	*blouse*
el melón	*cantaloupe*	**los pantalones**	*trousers, pants*
la papa	*potato*	**la corbata**	*necktie*
el tomate	*tomato*	**los guantes**	*gloves*
la carne	*meat*	**la falda**	*skirt*
la crema	*cream*	**los calcetines**	*socks*
el queso	*cheese*	**el disco**	*compact disc*
el rosbif	*roast beef*	**compacto**	
el bistec	*beefsteak*	**el radio**	*radio*
la uva	*grape*	**el supermercado**	*supermarket*
el jamón	*ham*	**el vestido**	*dress*
el chicle	*chewing gum*	**la camisa**	*shirt*
el estéreo	*stereo*	**el traje**	*suit*
la casete	*cassette, tape*		

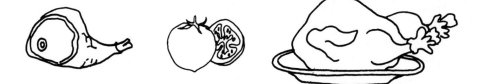

NEW WORDS

la sopa de tomate	*tomato soup*	el arroz	*rice*
la sopa de espárragos	*asparagus soup*	la chuleta de puerco	*pork chop*
la sopa de papas	*potato soup*	la cebolla	*onion*
el pollo	*chicken*	la lechuga	*lettuce*
la sopa de pollo	*chicken soup*	la verdura	*vegetable*
la mayonesa	*mayonnaise*	la leche	*milk*
el limón	*lemon*	muchas otras cosas	*many other things*
la naranja	*orange*	¿Qué venden?	*What do they sell?*
la manzana	*apple*	¿Qué medicinas venden?	*What medicines do they sell?*
la sal	*salt*	¿Qué come?	*What are you eating?*
la pimienta	*pepper (black)*		
el tocino	*bacon*		

13.8 CONVERSATION

Form groups of two students each and conduct a conversation. The following block will serve as a guide for your conversation. However, do not restrict yourself only to what is in the block.

What they sell in the supermarket, in the department store, in the music store

FIRST STUDENT: ¿Qué venden en la estación de gasolina?
SECOND STUDENT: Venden gasolina.
FIRST STUDENT: ¿Qué venden en el supermercado?
SECOND STUDENT: Venden carne, frutas, crema, leche, queso, mayonesa, sal, azúcar, pimienta y muchas otras cosas.
FIRST STUDENT: ¿Qué frutas venden en el supermercado?
SECOND STUDENT: Venden peras, uvas, fresas, limones, naranjas y muchas otras frutas.
FIRST STUDENT: ¿Qué carnes venden en el supermercado?
SECOND STUDENT: Venden rosbif, bistec, chuletas de puerco, jamón, tocino y muchas otras carnes.

FIRST STUDENT:	¿Qué verduras venden en el supermercado?
SECOND STUDENT:	Venden tomates, papas, espárragos, lechuga, cebollas y muchas otras verduras.
FIRST STUDENT:	¿Qué sopas venden en el supermercado?
SECOND STUDENT:	Venden sopa de tomate, sopa de papas, sopa de pollo, sopa de espárragos y muchas otras sopas.
FIRST STUDENT:	¿Qué venden en la tienda de ropa?
SECOND STUDENT:	Venden blusas, pantalones, guantes, faldas, vestidos, trajes, calcetines, corbatas, camisas y muchas otras cosas.
FIRST STUDENT:	¿Qué venden en la tienda de música?
SECOND STUDENT:	Venden radios, discos compactos, estéreos, cassettes y muchas otras cosas.

13.9 READING EXERCISE: ¡SIN MÁS NI MENOS!

In this lesson, you learned many new words for food and beverages. Now see if you can understand the following advertisement for a new food product and answer the questions that follow.

1. What do you think the word **sin** means?

   a. with   b. without   c. and

2. What clues in the advertisement helped you figure out the meaning of **sin**?

3. What do you think the word **jugo** means?

   a. juice   b. peel   c. jug

4. What clues in the advertisement helped you figure out the meaning of **jugo**?

5. Does this product contain sugar or NutraSweet?

13.10 WRITING EXERCISE

Imagine that you are hosting a dinner party for yourself and three friends. What will you serve? First write out a menu, then put together a shopping list of the items you will need to buy. Use vocabulary from this and previous lessons. Don't forget dessert!

VOCABULARY

NOUNS

el arroz	*rice*	**la pimienta**	*pepper (black)*
la cebolla	*onion*	**el pollo**	*chicken*
la chuleta de	*pork chop*	**la sal**	*salt*
puerco		**la sopa**	*soup*
la leche	*milk*	**la sopa de**	
la lechuga	*lettuce*	**espárragos**	*asparagus soup*
el limón	*lemon*	**la sopa de papas**	*potato soup*
la manzana	*apple*	**la sopa de pollo**	*chicken soup*
la mayonesa	*mayonnaise*	**la sopa de tomate**	*tomato soup*
la naranja	*orange*	**el tocino**	*bacon*
la persona	*person*	**la verdura**	*vegetable*

OTHER WORDS AND EXPRESSIONS

otro(a)	*other*	**¿Qué medicinas venden?**	*What medicines do they sell?*
muchas otras cosas.	*Many other things.*	**¿Qué come?**	*What are you eating?*
		¿Qué venden?	*What do they sell?*

LESSON 14

✵

¿Qué tiene usted?

- The verbs **tener, venir,** and **querer**
- Expressing likes with **gustar**
- Making introductions

Grammar: The present tense of **tener, venir,** and **querer**

tener *to have*

I have, I'm having	tengo	tenemos	we have, we're having
you have, you're having (fam.)	tienes	tenéis	you have, you're having (pl. fam.)
you have, you're having (formal)			you have, you're having (pl. formal)
he has, he's having	tiene	tienen	they have, they're having
she has, she's having			

venir *to come*

I come, I'm coming	vengo	venimos	we come, we're coming
you come, you're coming (fam.)	vienes	venís	you come, you're coming (pl. fam.)
you come, you're coming (formal)			you come, you're coming (pl. formal)
he comes, he's coming	viene	vienen	they come, they're coming
she comes, she's coming			

querer *to want*

I want	quiero	queremos	we want
you want (fam.)	quieres	queréis	you want (pl. fam.)
you want (formal)			you want (pl. formal)
he wants	quiere	quieren	they want
she wants			

EXAMPLES: —**Tengo dos libros.**   *I have two books.*
—**¿Cuántos tienes tú?**   *How many do you have?*
—**Tengo tres libros,**
     pero quiero cuatro.   *I have three books, but I want four.*
—**¿Vienes a la fiesta?**   *Are you coming to the party?*

Notice that the verbs **tener**, querer, and **venir** are irregular verbs. Although they use the same endings in the present tense as regular -**er** and -**ir** verbs, they have an internal change. **The e** in the first syllable of the verb changes to **ie** in all forms except the first and second person plural. Notice also that the first person singular of venir and tener is like the first person singular of **salir** (**salgo**).

14.1 THE GARDEN TERRACE

el gato	*cat*	valiente	*brave (masc., fem.)*
el perro	*dog*	Tengo...	*I have...*
el toro	*bull*	No tengo...	*I don't have...*
la terraza	*terrace*	¿Tiene usted?	*Have you...? Do you*
el trabajo	*job, work*		*have...?*
el pájaro	*bird*	No sé.	*I don't know.*

14.2 LISTENING EXERCISE

Repeat each sentence after your instructor says it, reading along in the book as you speak.

1. Tengo muchos libros.
2. Tengo un gato.
3. Tengo la llave.
4. Tengo una bicicleta.
5. Tengo un paraguas.
6. Quiero un perro.
7. No quiero un tigre.
8. No quiero un toro.
9. Quiero un piano.
10. No quiero una guitarra.

11. ¿Tiene usted un perro?

12. ¿Tiene usted la llave?

13. ¿Tiene usted un gato?

14. ¿Quiere usted un pájaro?

15. ¿Quieren ustedes un toro?

16. ¿Quiere usted un tigre?

17. El doctor tiene un auto.

18. Roberto tiene una bicicleta.

19. El canario es un pájaro.

20. El toro es valiente.

14.3 ORAL EXERCISE

Answer the following questions.

1. ¿Tiene usted muchos discos compactos de música mexicana?

2. ¿Tiene usted muchos libros?

3. ¿Tiene usted un perro?

4. ¿Tiene usted un gato?

5. ¿Tiene usted las llaves para la casa?

6. ¿Quiere usted un pájaro?

7. ¿Quiere usted un perro?

8. ¿Quiere usted un auto?

9. ¿Quiere usted una bicicleta?

10. ¿Tiene usted un paraguas?

11. ¿Tiene usted una bicicleta?

12. ¿Tiene usted un canario?

13. ¿Viene usted a la fiesta este fin de semana?

14. ¿Viene su familia a la universidad mañana?

15. ¿Viene usted a clase a tiempo?

16. ¿Viene usted a clase tarde?

Can you do this exercise with your book closed?

14.4 ORAL OR WRITTEN EXERCISE

Change the following statements into questions in the **usted** form.

EXAMPLE: **Tengo un gato.**
ANSWER: **¿Tiene usted un gato?**

1. Tengo una bicicleta.

2. Tengo muchos discos compactos.

3. Quiero una guitarra.

4. Tengo la llave.

5. Quiero un perro.   9. Tengo un gato blanco.
6. Quiero un auto.   10. Quiero un estéreo.
7. Vengo a clase temprano mañana. 11. Vengo a tu casa tarde el sábado.
8. Vengo a la fiesta el viernes.

14.5 ORAL OR WRITTEN EXERCISE

Answer the following questions.

1. ¿Tiene un paraguas? ¿Dónde está?   8. ¿Viene usted a la iglesia el domingo?
2. ¿Dónde está su familia?   9. ¿Tiene usted un gato?
3. ¿Tiene un pájaro en casa?   10. ¿Tiene usted un radio?
4. ¿Quiere usted un perro?   11. ¿Quiere usted un café?
5. ¿Tiene usted un perro? ¿Dónde está? 12. ¿Tiene usted un libro de español?
6. ¿Quiere usted un avión?   13. ¿Tiene usted un canario?
7. ¿Tiene usted un estéreo?   14. ¿Viene usted a clase mañana?

Grammar: The present tense of the verb **creer**

creer *to think, to believe (an opinion)*			
I think, I'm thinking	creo	creemos	*we think, we're thinking*
you think, you're thinking (fam.)	crees	creéis	*you think, you're thinking (pl. fam.)*
you think, you're thinking (formal)			*you think, you're thinking (pl. formal)*
he thinks, he's thinking	cree	creen	*they think, they're thinking*
she thinks, she's thinking			

EXAMPLES: —¿**Qué crees del trabajo?** *What do you think of the work?*
—**Creo que es interesante.** *I think it's interesting.*

14.6 EVERYDAY EXPRESSIONS

Creo que es interesante.	*I think that it's interesting.*	**Por favor.**	*Please.*
¿Qué cree?	*What do you think?*	**¿Cree?**	*Do you think so?*
Creo que sí.	*I think so.*	**¿Crees?**	*Do you think so? (fam.)*
Creo que no.	*I don't think so.*	**No tengo tiempo.**	*I don't have time.*

Grammar: Adjective placement

Remember: Adjectives usually go *after* nouns in Spanish. We do not say black cat. Instead, we say cat black (**gato negro**) or a garden beautiful (**un jardín lindo**).

14.7 LISTENING EXERCISE

Listen to the following composition as your instructor reads it aloud. Read along in your book, paying particular attention to the pronunciation of the Spanish words.

Alberto y su familia

Alberto vive en Bogotá, la capital de Colombia, con su familia. Alberto es muy simpático y muy inteligente. Estudia inglés en la universidad y habla muy bien. Escribe composiciones para la clase de inglés. En casa, Alberto habla español con su mamá y su papá.

El papá de Alberto trabaja en un banco y su mamá trabaja en un hospital.

Alberto tiene muchos discos compactos porque tiene una colección de música americana. Le gusta la música americana. Tiene muchos libros americanos también.

El papá de Alberto tiene un auto. Alberto tiene una bicicleta. Todos los días, el papá y la mamá de Alberto van al trabajo en su auto. Alberto va a la universidad en su bicicleta.

En la casa de Alberto hay un jardín lindo. Hay un canario y muchas flores en el jardín. El canario canta todo el día. En el jardín también hay muchas plantas tropicales.

14.8 ORAL EXERCISE

Read each sentence in the composition above and translate it into English.

14.9 READING EXERCISE

Now read aloud a whole paragraph of the composition. Try to read as smoothly as you can.

14.10 ORAL OR WRITTEN MINI-TEST (OPTIONAL)

Answer these questions to see how well you understood the composition.

1.   ¿Dónde vive Alberto?
2.   ¿Es inteligente Alberto?
3.   ¿Es simpático Alberto?
4.   ¿Habla inglés Alberto?
5.   ¿Habla español Alberto?
6.   ¿Dónde trabaja el papá de Alberto?
7.   ¿Dónde trabaja la mamá de Alberto?
8.   ¿Tiene discos compactos Alberto?
9.   ¿Tiene Alberto un auto?
10. ¿Va a la universidad Alberto?
11. ¿Tiene un gato Alberto?
12. ¿Hay flores en el jardín de la casa de Alberto y su familia?

Grammar: Expressing likes and dislikes with **gustar**

To say you like or dislike one thing (singular), use **gusta**.

EXAMPLES:

Me gusta el baloncesto.	*I like basketball.*
¿Te gusta el baloncesto?	*Do you like basketball?*
A Alberto le gusta el baloncesto también.	*Alberto likes basketball, too.*
Nos gusta el baloncesto.	*We like basketball.*
A mis amigos no les gusta el baloncesto.	*My friends don't like basketball.*

To express like or dislike of more than one thing, use **gustan**.

EXAMPLES:

Me gustan las flores.	*I like flowers.*
¿Te gustan las plantas?	*Do you like plants?*

> A Susana no le gustan las novelas. *Susana doesn't like novels.*
> Nos gustan los poemas también. *We like poems also.*
> A mis amigos no les gustan los poemas. *My friends don't like poems.*

Notice that you used different words with **gusta** and **gustan**, depending on who is doing the liking or disliking. Use these forms to talk about likes and dislikes.

Who likes /dislikes?		One thing	More than one thing
I like	me	gusta	gustan
I don't like	no me	gusta	gustan
You like (fam.)	te	gusta	gustan
You don't like (fam.)	no te	gusta	gustan
you like (formal)	le	gusta	gustan
he likes	le	gusta	gustan
she likes	le	gusta	gustan
you don't like (formal)	no le	gusta	gustan
he doesn't like	no le	gusta	gustan
she doesn't like	no le	gusta	gustan
we like	nos	gusta	gustan
we don't like	no nos	gusta	gustan
you like (pl. formal)	les	gusta	gustan
they like	les	gusta	gustan
you don't like	no les	gusta	gustan
they don't like (pl. formal)	no les	gusta	gustan

14.11 ORAL EXERCISE

Say whether you like or dislike the following items.

EXAMPLE: **las papas**
ANSWER: **Me gustan las papas.**
        No me gustan las papas.

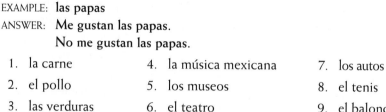

1. la carne
2. el pollo
3. las verduras

4. la música mexicana
5. los museos
6. el teatro

7. los autos americanos
8. el tenis
9. el baloncesto

Grammar: **Gustar** with infinitives

If you want to talk about what you like or don't like *to do*, use **gusta** plus an infinitive.

Me gusta nadar.	*I like to swim.*
¿Te gusta jugar tenis?	*Do you like to play tennis?*
A mi amiga no le gusta estudiar.	*My friend doesn't like to study.*
Nos gusta leer novelas.	*We like to read novels.*
No les gusta escribir cartas.	*They don't like to write letters.*

Also notice that when you use **le** or **les** with **gustar**, it isn't always clear who likes or dislikes the thing you're talking about. To clarify, use a plus the person's name or another word that tells who the person is: **a María, a la profesora, a mi familia, a mis amigos,** etc.

EXAMPLES:

A Elena le gusta leer.	*Elena likes to read.*
A mis amigos les gusta nadar.	*My friends like to swim.*

14.12   ORAL OR WRITTEN EXERCISE

Create sentences using the words from each column to talk about people's likes and dislikes. Feel free to add more items to the third column.

		los autos modernos
		la música chilena
Me		ir al cine
Le		las manzanas
Nos	gusta	las flores
Les	gustan	ir en bicicleta
A...		estudiar
		las novelas
		los poemas

14.13 CONVERSATION VOCABULARY (OPTIONAL)

la escuela	*school*	muchos	*many patients*
para tu clase	*for your class*	pacientes	
¿Quieres ir?	*Do you want to go?*	tomar un café	*to have coffee*
y	*and*	Vivo en...	*I live in...*
la misma clase	*the same class*	¿Quieres ir con	*Do you want to go*
todo el tiempo	*all the time*	nosotros?	*with us?*
para practicar	*in order to practice*	¡Cómo no!	*Of course!*
Mucho gusto.	*Pleased to meet you.*	Le presento a	*Allow me to introduce*
El gusto es mío.	*The pleasure is mine.*	un(a) amigo(a).	*a friend. (formal)*
Un placer.	*A pleasure.*	Te presento a	*Allow me to introduce a*
		un(a) amigo(a).	*friend. (fam.)*

Introducing a friend with **tú**

FIRST STUDENT: **Te presento a un amigo, Alberto García. Susana Smith.** *Allow me to introduce a friend, Alberto García. Susana Smith.*

SECOND STUDENT: **Mucho gusto.** *Pleased to meet you.*

THIRD STUDENT: **Mucho gusto.** *Pleased to meet you.*

Introducing an acquaintance with **usted**

FIRST STUDENT: **Le presento al Sr. García. Srta. Torres.** *Allow me to introduce you to Sr. García. Srta. Torres.*

SECOND STUDENT: **Un placer.** *A pleasure.*

THIRD STUDENT: **El gusto es mío.** *The pleasure is mine*

14.14 CONVERSATION (OPTIONAL)

Your instructor will call on students to take the roles of Juan, Susana and Alberto, or those of Sr. García, Srta. Torres and Sr. Rivas. One student will introduce the other two to each other.

The following block will serve as a guide for your conversation. However, do not restrict yourself only to what is in the block.

Meeting a friend

JUAN: Susana, te presento a un amigo. Alberto García, Susana Smith.
SUSANA: Mucho gusto.
ALBERTO: Mucho gusto.
JUAN: Susana está en mi clase de español.
SUSANA: Alberto, ¿dónde vives?
ALBERTO: Vivo en Bogotá. ¿Y tú?
SUSANA: Vivo aquí cerca de la universidad.
JUAN: Susana y yo estudiamos en la misma clase. Estudiamos mucho. Nos gusta hablar español. Hablamos en español todo el tiempo, para practicar.
ALBERTO: ¿Susana, escribes composiciones en español para tu clase?
SUSANA: Sí, Juan y yo escribimos composiciones todo el tiempo para practicar.
JUAN: Susana, Alberto y yo vamos al cine. ¿Quieres ir con nosotros?
SUSANA: Sí, ¡cómo no! Muchas gracias.

Meeting an acquaintance

SR. RIVAS: Le presento al Sr. García. Srta. Torres.
SRTA. TORRES: Un placer.
SR. GARCÍA: El gusto es mío.
SRTA. TORRES: ¿Trabaja usted cerca de aquí?
SR. GARCÍA: Sí, trabajo en el hospital. Soy doctor. Tengo muchos pacientes.
SR. RIVAS: Sr. García, vamos a tomar un café. ¿Quiere usted venir?
SR. GARCÍA: Sí, ¡cómo no!

14.15 READING EXERCISE: ÚNICOS Y SIN PELAMBRE

In this lesson, you learned the words for various kinds of animals. The following text and photo is the introduction to an article about a very special kind of Mexican dog. With the help of the words provided, read the text, look at the photo, and answer the questions that follow.

Hay perros de perros. Pero estos ni tienen pelo ni comen carne.

ÚNICOS
Y SIN PELAMBRE

Son vegetarianos y no son producto de la imaginación. Existen, tienen poderes medicinales, son utilizados como bolsas de agua caliente y hace siglos los aztecas y los incas los adoran como a sus dioses.

pero	*but*
pelo	*hair*
poderes	*powers*

1. Do these dogs have hair?
2. What do they eat?
3. What kind of powers do they have?

Now see if you can match the following phrases from the text with their English equivalents on the right.

1. ni tienen pelo ni comen carne   a. they are used

2. no son producto de
   la imaginación   b. neither have hair nor eat meat

3. los aztecas y los incas los
   adoran como a sus dioses   c. they are vegetarians

4. son utilizados   d. they are not a product of the
                                         imagination

5. son vegetarianos   e. the Aztecs and the Incas worship
                                         them like gods

14.15 WRITING EXERCISE

You just finished reading an article about some Mexican dogs. In your opinion, what is the ideal pet? Write six to eight sentences in Spanish describing your ideal pet, what it does, what it eats, and what it looks like.

VOCABULARY

NOUNS

el gato	*cat*	el pájaro	*bird*
el toro	*bull*	el perro	*dog*
el trabajo	*job, work*	la terraza	*terrace*

VERBS

creer	*To think, to believe*	tener	*to have*
gustar	*To like*	venir	*to come*
querer	*To want*		

ADJECTIVES

valiente	*brave (masc. fem.)*

OTHER WORDS AND EXPRESSIONS

¿Crees?	*Do you think so?* *(fam.)*	No sé.	*I don't know.*
¿Cree?	*Do you think so?* *(formal)*	No tengo tiempo.	*I don't have time.*
		Por favor.	*Please.*
		¿Qué cree?	*What do you think?* *(formal)*
Creo que es interesante.	*I think that it's interesting.*	Creo que no. Creo que sí.	*I don't think so* *I think so.*

OPTIONAL LIST

NOUNS

la escuela	*school*

ADJECTIVES

mismo(a)	*same*

OTHER WORDS AND EXPRESSIONS

¡Cómo no!	*Of course!*	¿Quieres ir (con nosotros)?	*Do you want to go (with us)?*
El gusto es mío.	*The pleasure is mine.*	para practicar para tu clase	*in order to practice for your class*
Te presento a un(a) amigo(a).	*Allow me to introduce a friend. (fam.)*	Le presento a un(a) amigo(a).	*Allow me to introduce a friend. (formal)*
todo el tiempo	*all the time*	Mucho gusto.	*Pleased to meet you.*
tomar un café	*to have coffee and*	muchos pacientes	*many patients*
Un placer.	*A pleasure.*		
y	*and*		

LESSON 15

¿ Te gusta la música?
- The present tense of **tocar, cantar,** and **tomar**
- Forming adverbs with **-mente**
- Numbers 13–1,000, 1,000–1,000,000
- More on telling time

Grammar: The verbs **tocar, cantar,** and **tomar**

tocar *to play (an instrument)*			
I play, I'm playing	toco	tocamos	*we play, we're playing*
you play, you're playing (fam.)	tocas	tocáis	*you play, you're playing (pl. fam.)*
you play, you're playing (formal)			*you play, you're playing (pl. formal)*
he plays, he's playing	toca	tocan	*they play, they're playing*
she plays, she's playing			

cantar *to sing*	
canto	cantamos
cantas	cantáis
canta	cantan

tomar *to take*	
tomo	tomamos
tomas	tomáis
toma	toman

EXAMPLES: —¿Tocas la guitarra?   *Do you (fam.) play the guitar?*
—Sí. Canto canciones   *Yes. I also sing Mexican songs.*
mexicanas también.

In English, you say *I drink coffee* and *I eat soup*. In Spanish you say *I take coffee* (**Tomo café**) and *I take soup* (**Tomo sopa**). The verb **tomar** (*to take*) is used to express drinking and eating liquids like soup. To express eating solid foods use the verb **comer** (*to eat*). You may also use the verb **beber** (*to drink*) to express the idea of drinking. Usages of **beber** and **tomar** vary regionally.

15.1 BY THE LIGHT OF THE MOON

la luz	*light*	el (la) guitarrista	*the guitar player*
la luna	*moon*	la canción	*song*
a la luz de la luna	*by the light of the moon*	las canciones mexicanas	*Mexican songs*
simpático(a)	*nice*	absolutamente	*absolutely*
el (la) pianista	*the pianist*	o	*or*

15.2 LISTENING EXERCISE

Repeat each sentence after your instructor says it, reading along in the book as you speak.

1. El pianista toca el piano.
2. El guitarrista toca la guitarra.
3. ¿Toca Ud. la guitarra?
4. ¿Tocan Uds. el piano?
5. No cantamos en la clase.
6. Whitney Houston canta muy bien.
7. Los estudiantes no cantan en la clase.
8. Los estudiantes hablan español en la clase.
9. Plácido Domingo canta canciones lindas.
10. ¿Ud. canta también?
11. Mi mejor amigo es muy simpático.
12. Su mamá es muy simpática
13. Tomo sopa para la cena.
14. Bebo leche con la cena.
15. Como bistec para la cena.
16. Tomo la cena en casa.

15.3 ORAL EXERCISE

Answer the following questions.

1. ¿Canta usted mucho?
2. ¿Canta usted canciones mexicanas?
3. ¿Cantan mucho sus amigos?
4. ¿Canta mucho su mejor amigo?
5. ¿Canta mucho su mejor amiga?
6. ¿Es simpático(a) su compañero(a) de cuarto?
7. ¿Es simpática la mamá de su mejor amigo?
8. ¿Toca usted la guitarra?
9. ¿Toca usted el piano?
10. ¿Toca la guitarra Eric Clapton?
11. ¿Toca el piano Elton John?
12. ¿Dónde toma usted la cena?
13. ¿Qué toma usted para la cena?
14. ¿Toma usted sopa para la cena?
15. ¿Toma usted rosbif para la cena?
16. ¿Toma usted café para la cena?
17. ¿Toma usted bistec para la cena?
18. ¿Toma usted la cena por la noche?

Can you answer the questions above with your book closed?

15.4 ORAL OR WRITTEN EXERCISE

Give the correct form of the following adjectives. Follow the example.

EXAMPLE: **blanco/la luna**
ANSWER: **la luna blanca** (*sing. fem.*)

1. bonito/los canarios
2. lindo la luna
3. simpático/las amigas
4. chiquito/los gatos
5. delicioso/la sopa
6. solo/los guitarristas
7. cubano/las canciones
8. mexicano/la pianista

15.5 ORAL OR WRITTEN EXERCISE

Give the **we** form (first person plural) of the following verbs.

EXAMPLE: **trabaja**
ANSWER: **trabajamos**

1. habla   6. compra
2. estudia   7. toca
3. toma   8. prepara
4. nada   9. está
5. progresa   10. va

15.6 ORAL OR WRITTEN EXERCISE

Answer the following questions.

1. ¿Qué toma usted para la cena?
2. ¿Toma usted muchas cosas para la cena?
3. ¿Toma usted la cena en casa o en un restaurante?
4. ¿Habla usted español en la clase?
5. ¿Toca usted el piano?
6. ¿Toca usted la guitarra?
7. ¿Canta usted mucho?
8. Generalmente, ¿cuándo canta usted?
9. ¿Canta por la mañana o por la noche?
10. ¿Es simpático su compañero de cuarto?
11. ¿Toma usted sopa para la cena?
12. ¿Es bonita la luna?
13. ¿Es delicioso el rosbif?
14. ¿Tiene usted un perro?

Grammar: Forming adverbs with **-mente**

To form adverbs, add **-mente** to adjectives.

ADJECTIVES		ADVERBS	
posible	*possible*	**posiblemente**	*possibly*
probable	*probable*	**probablemente**	*probably*
general	*general*	**generalmente**	*generally*
final	*final*	**finalmente**	*finally*
natural	*natural*	**naturalmente**	*naturally*

However, when an adjective ends in **-o**, change the **-o** to **-a**, and then add **-mente**.

absoluto	*absolute*	**absolutamente**	*absolutely*
completo	*complete*	**completamente**	*completely*

Note: You will say these words correctly if you say the adjectives first, and then add -mente. Like this: **general-mente, natural-mente, final-mente, probable-mente.**

EXAMPLES:

Generalmente canto por la noche.	*I generally sing at night.*
Probablemente tomamos la cena a las ocho.	*We will probably eat, dinner at eight.*

15.7 ORAL OR WRITTEN EXERCISE

Combine the words in the four columns to form complete sentences about your and other's food preferences and meals.

I	II	III	IV
Generalmente	tomo	café	para la cena
Raramente		un sándwich (de...)	
Frecuentemente	no tomo	sopa (de...)	
Normalmente		una ensalada	para el desayuno
	mi amigo toma	carne	
		jamón	para el almuerzo
	mi amiga toma	rosbif	
		bistec	
		chocolate	
		leche	
		queso	
		papas	
		macarrones	
		pizza	

Grammar: The **Usted** form

Remember that the you form of every verb actually means eight things.

EXAMPLE:

Toma...   *You take...*   *¿Toma...?*   *Do you take...?*
          He takes...   *Does he take...?*
          She takes...   *Does she take...?*
          It takes...   *Does it take...?*

Grammar: The verb **jugar**

The verb **jugar** also means *to play*, but it refers to playing a sport or game, while tocar refers to playing music or an instrument.

jugar *to play (a game)*	
juego	jugamos
juegas	jugáis
juega	juegan

Notice that the first person plural form (**jugamos**) and the second person plural form (**jugáis**) are the only forms that do not add an -e to the stem (**jug-**). You need to memorize these forms, since they don't completely follow the normal rules.

EXAMPLES: **Juego fútbol y toco el piano.**   *I play football and I play piano.*
          ¿Qué juegos?   *What (sport) do you play?*
          ¿Qué instrumento musical tocas?   *What musical instrument do you play?*

15.8 ORAL EXERCISE

Ask a classmate questions with **jugar** or **tocar**, using the activities provided and following the examples.

EXAMPLE: **tenis**
ANSWER: **¿Te gusta jugar tenis?**
EXAMPLE: **la música mexicana**
ANSWER: **¿Te gusta tocar la música mexicana?**

1. baloncesto
2. fútbol
3. el piano
4. el violín
5. tenis
6. la música popular
7. Monopoly
8. la guitarra
9. la música clásica
10. béisbol

15.9 CONVERSATION VOCABULARY

el cereal	*cereal*	la taza de café	*cup of coffee*
el jugo	*juice*	el postre	*dessert*
el jugo de tomate	*tomato juice*	el coctel de frutas	*fruit cocktail*
el jugo de naranja	*orange juice*	a veces	*sometimes*
el pan tostado	*toast*	después de la cena	*after dinner*
el huevo frito	*fried egg*	Veo un programa de televisión.	*I'm watching/I watch television program.*
el tostador eléctrico	*electric toaster*	¿Qué tomas?	*What do you have? (fam.) (food, drink)?*
el desayuno	*breakfast*		
el almuerzo	*lunch*	¿Qué haces?	*What do you do? What are you doing? (fam.)*
la cena	*supper, evening meal*		

📼 15.10 CONVERSATION

The following block will serve as a guide to your conversation. However, do
not restrict yourself only to what is in the block.

Breakfast, lunch, and dinner

FIRST STUDENT: ¿Qué tomas para el desayuno?

SECOND STUDENT: Tomo jugo de naranja, café, pan tostado y un huevo
frito. ¿Y tú?

FIRST STUDENT: Tomo leche, un cereal y pan tostado.

SECOND STUDENT: ¿Tienes un tostador?

FIRST STUDENT: Sí, tengo un tostador eléctrico.

SECOND STUDENT: ¿A qué hora tomas el desayuno?

FIRST STUDENT: A las siete. ¿Y tú?

SECOND STUDENT: También a las siete.

FIRST STUDENT: ¿Qué tomas para el almuerzo?

SECOND STUDENT: Tomo sopa, un sándwich, leche o una taza de café.

FIRST STUDENT: ¿Qué tomas para la cena?

SECOND STUDENT: Tomo carne, verduras, una ensalada y postre.

FIRST STUDENT: ¿No tomas un coctel de frutas?

SECOND STUDENT: A veces.

FIRST STUDENT: ¿Qué haces después de la cena?

SECOND STUDENT: Veo un programa de televisión. ¿Y tú?

FIRST STUDENT: Estudio en casa.

Grammar: Expressing large quantities

1	uno	12	doce
2	dos	13	trece
3	tres	14	catorce
4	cuatro	15	quince
5	cinco	16	dieciséis
6	seis	17	diecisiete
7	siete	18	dieciocho
8	ocho	19	diecinueve
9	nueve	20	veinte
10	diez	21	veintiuno
11	once	22	veintidós

23	veintitrés	100	cien
24	veinticuatro	101	ciento uno (etc.)
25	veinticinco	200	doscientos
26	veintiséis	201	doscientos uno (etc.)
27	veintisiete	300	trescientos
28	veintiocho	301	trescientos uno (etc.)
29	veintinueve	400	cuatrocientos
30	treinta	401	cuatrocientos uno (etc.)
31	treinta y uno (etc.)	500	quinientos
40	cuarenta	600	seiscientos
41	cuarenta y uno (etc.)	700	setecientos
50	cincuenta	800	ochocientos
51	cincuenta y uno (etc.)	900	novecientos
60	sesenta	1.000	mil
61	sesenta y uno (etc.)	2.000	dos mil
70	setenta	3.000	tres mil
71	setenta y uno (etc.)	10.000	diez mil
80	ochenta	20.000	veinte mil
81	ochenta y uno (etc.)	100.000	cien mil
90	noventa	200.000	doscientos mil
91	noventa y uno (etc.)	1.000.000	un millón
		2.000.000	dos millones

EXAMPLES:

Tengo veintiocho dólares ¿y tú?   *I have twenty-eight dollars. And you?*
¡Qué bueno! Tengo cincuenta y dos.   *That's great! I have fifty-two.*

15.11 ORAL OR WRITTEN EXERCISE

What number in Spanish correctly expresses the quantity or number indicated? Follow the example.

EXAMPLE: **number of days in a year**
ANSWER: **trescientos sesenta y cinco**

1. the year you were born
2. the number of days in February
3. the number of pennies in a dollar
4. the number of nickels in a dollar
5. your age
6. your height in inches
7. the tuition (per semester) at your school
8. the amount of money in your wallet
9. the number of hours in a day
10. the number of hours in a week
11. 20 x 10,000 = ?
12. 30 x 100,000 = ?

Grammar: More on telling time

Now that you've learned all the numbers, you can tell time precisely. For minutes after the hour, use **y**. For minutes before the hour, use **menos**.

EXAMPLES:

Son las dos y veinticinco.   *It's two twenty-five.*
Son las cuatro menos veinte.   *It's twenty to four.*
Son las tres y cuarenta.   *It's three-forty.*

15.12 ORAL OR WRITTEN EXERCISE

Say what time each clock is showing.

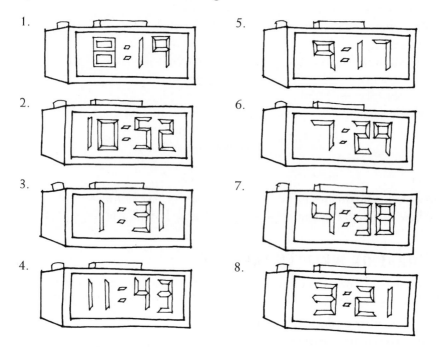

1.
2.
3.
4.
5.
6.
7.
8.

15.13 READING EXERCISE: ¡VIVA LA MÚSICA ROMÁNTICA!

Look at the following program listing for El Romántico 89.7, a Spanish-language radio station. Look at the descriptions of its music and programs, then answer the questions that follow.

Programación
La programación de EL ROMÁNTICO FM, 89.7 consiste de los hits de la música romántica — moderna, simpática y siempre muy, muy romántica.

La Mañana Fresca
La buena combinación musical se inicia por la mañana, con Juan Francisco Lamonte, de 7:00 AM a 12:00 PM, donde el público escucha lo mejor de la música romántica en conjunción con llamadas telefónicas. Todos los días.

Baladas del Mediodía
Las más lindas baladas de hoy y del pasado, de 12:00 m a 2:00 PM, bajo la conducción de Alfonso Reyes. De lunes a viernes.

La Tarde Divertida
La música más emocionante del mundo romántico, bajo la conducción de Carlos Manuel Thomas, de 2:00 PM a 7:00 PM. Todos los días.

Romance
La música más suave y romántica del mundo musical, a través de Bernie Elías y el Programa Romance. De 9:00 PM a 11:00 PM. Lunes a viernes.

Tres en Concierto
(José José, Luis Miguel y su invitado)
Un concierto para el amor y la pasión. Con Alfonso Reyes, de 8:00 PM a 10:00 PM. Todos los domingos.

Un Break Musical
Dos canciones en inglés, una en español con Ramiro Mota, de 7:00 a 9:00 PM todos los domingos.

Una Diversión Nocturnal
Este fabuloso programa, con lo mejor de la música de los años 70's y 80's, está a cargo de nuestro director general Tito Mendoza, los domingos de 10:00 PM a 12:00 de la medianoche.

1. ¿A qué hora tocan la música de los años 70 y 80? ¿Cómo se llama el programa?

2. ¿A qué hora tocan baladas lindas?

3. ¿Quién es el conductor de La Tarde Divertida? ¿A qué hora es el programa?

4. ¿Cuándo es posible escuchar música en inglés? ¿Cómo se llama el programa?

5. ¿Quién es el director general de la estación de radio? ¿A qué hora es su programa?

6. ¿En qué programa es posible escuchar llamadas telefónicas? ¿A qué hora es este programa?

7. ¿A qué hora es posible escuchar un concierto? ¿Qué concierto tocan esta semana?

15.14 WRITING EXERCISE

What kind of music do you like to listen to? Write six to eight sentences in Spanish describing what kind of music you listen to and when. Why do you like that music? What music don't you like? You may choose words from the following list to use in your description.

(No) Me gusta la música...   porque es....
    alternativa   emocionante
    rock   interesante
    jazz   excelente
    rap   estúpida
    hip-hop   aburrida *(boring)*
    clásica   experimental
    folklórica   original
    mexicana   tradicional
    cubana   diferente

VOCABULARY

NOUNS

el almuerzo	*lunch*	el jugo de naranja	*orange juice*
la canción	*song*	el jugo de tomate	*tomato juice*
la cena	*dinner*	la luna	*moon*
el cereal	*cereal*	la luz	*light*
el coctel de frutas	*fruit cocktail*	el pan	*bread*
el desayuno	*breakfast*	el pan tostado	*toast*
el (la) guitarrista	*the guitar player*	el (la) pianista	*the pianist*
el huevo	*egg*	el postre	*dessert*
el huevo frito	*fried egg*	la taza de café	*cup of coffee*
el jugo	*juice*	el tostador eléctrico	*electric toaster*

VERBS

cantar	*to sing*	tocar	*to play (music, an instrument)*
jugar	*to play (a sport, a game)*	tomar	*to take, to drink*

ADJECTIVES

absoluto	*absolute*	natural	*natural*
completo	*complete*	posible	*posible*
final	*final*	probable	*probable*
general	*general*	simpático(a)	*nice*

OTHER WORDS AND EXPRESSIONS

a la luz de	*by the light of*	**posiblemente**	*possibly*
la luna	*the moon*	**probablemente**	*probably*
a veces	*sometimes*	**¿Qué tomas?**	*What do you have? (fam.)*
absolutamente	*absolutely*	**¿Qué haces?**	*What do you do? What*
completamente	*completely*		*are you doing? (fam.)*
después de	*after*	**Veo un programa**	*I watch a television*
finalmente	*finally*	**de televisión.**	*program.*
generalmente	*generally*	**naturalmente**	*naturally*

LESSON 16

✳

De visita en México
• Talking about Mexico

 **16.1 MEXICO**

el (la) músico	*musician*	como	*such as*
la gente	*people*	rico(a)	*tasty, rich*
la montaña alta	*high mountain*	la enchilada	*enchilada (Mexican dish*
el país	*country, nation*		*with tortillas, filling,*
el hombre	*man*		*and sauce)*
romántico(a)	*romantic*	el taco	*taco (tortilla filled with*
la piscina	*swimming pool*		*meat, fish, or*
la mujer	*woman*		*vegetables)*
el valle	*valley*	la quesadilla	*quesadilla (toasted tortilla*
el entusiasmo	*enthusiasm*		*with cheese)*
la comida	*food*		

🔲 16.2 LISTENING EXERCISE

Repeat each sentence after your instructor says it, reading along in the book as you speak.

1. Los músicos tocan sus guitarras.
2. Hablan con mucho entusiasmo.
3. México es un país muy interesante.
4. Hay montañas altas y valles inmensos.
5. Toman café.
6. Hay mucha comida rica.
7. Los mexicanos son muy simpáticos.
8. Cantan canciones románticas.
9. Los mexicanos bailan (dance) en las fiestas.
10. Los turistas nadan en las piscinas y bailan en las terrazas.

🔲 16.3 LISTENING EXERCISE

Listen to the following composition as your instructor reads it aloud.

México

México es un país interesante. En México hay montañas altas y valles inmensos.

Los mexicanos son muy simpáticos. En las fiestas hablan con mucho entusiasmo y bailan la música mexicana. Los músicos tocan sus guitarras y cantan canciones románticas. La gente canta y baila. Hay mucha comida rica, como enchiladas, tacos, y quesadillas.

Los hoteles mexicanos son modernos. Muchos hoteles tienen terrazas grandes y piscinas. Los turistas nadan en las piscinas y bailan en las terrazas. Generalmente hay guitarristas en los hoteles. Los guitarristas tocan las guitarras y cantan canciones para los turistas. En México hay muchas casas bonitas. Unas casas tienen jardines. En los jardines hay pájaros lindos y plantas tropicales.

16.4 ORAL EXERCISE

Read each sentence in the composition above and translate it into English.

16.5 READING EXERCISE

Now read aloud a whole paragraph of the composition. Try to read as smoothly as you can.

16.6 ORAL OR WRITTEN MINI-TEST (OPTIONAL)

Answer these questions to see how well you understood the composition.

1. ¿Es México un país interesante?
2. ¿Hay montañas altas en México?
3. ¿Hay valles inmensos en México?
4. ¿Són simpáticos los mexicanos?
5. ¿Toman café los mexicanos?
6. ¿Cantan canciones los mexicanos?
7. ¿Tocan sus guitarras?
8. ¿Hay comida rica en las fiestas?
9. ¿Qué comida hay en las fiestas?
10. ¿Tienen terrazas en los hoteles?
11. ¿Tienen piscinas los hoteles?
12. ¿Son románticos los mexicanos?
13. ¿Son grandes las piscinas?
14. ¿Nadan los turistas?
15. ¿Bailan en las terrazas?
16. ¿Hay pájaros lindos en México?
17. ¿Hay plantas tropicales en México?

16.9 READING EXERCISE: MÉXICO DESCONOCIDO

In this lesson you learned about Mexico. Since you'd like to learn more about this country, you decide to subscribe to the magazine **México desconocido**. Read the following advertisement, then answer the questions that follow.

Estimado lector:

En este momento está usted leyendo y disfrutando de un ejemplar de **México desconocido**, por eso le estamos haciendo una invitación para suscribirse doblemente.

México desconocido es una revista que por más de **quince años** se ha dedicado a visitar los lugares más recónditos del país para darlos a conocer a sus lectores a través de sus artículos y reportajes mensuales.

Por eso, ahora, como una promoción especial, al suscribirse recibirá también las seis guías de Ediciones Especiales que salgan en el año que esté suscrito. Estas guías están dedicadas a un tema específico, y en ellas usted encontrará información completa y actualizada de las playas que puede visitar, las ciudades coloniales que tanto nos enorgullecen, los parques y reservas ecológicas del país, y otros temas.

Además, cada guía contiene datos históricos, fechas importantes, mapas de localización, explicaciones, fotografías, sugerencias para su visita y un índice toponímico para ubicar más fácilmente el lugar que le interese visitar. Usted sólo paga **$150,000** y recibe mensualmente por un año la revista **México desconocido** y cada dos meses la nueva guía de Ediciones Especiales, directamente en su domicilio.

Ahora bien, si usted no desea esta doble suscripción, pague **$84,000** por una suscripción en lugar de **$96,000** por un año y ahorre **$12,000**.

Además, al suscribirse tendrá la oportunidad de participar en nuestro gran sorteo de **XV ANIVERSARIO** con **20 premios** por un valor de más de **$25'000,000** de pesos.

(Busque las bases en esta revista).

1. How old is **México desconocido**?
2. What type of information do the **Ediciones Especiales** contain?
3. How much does it cost (in pesos) to subscribe to **México desconocido** and the **Ediciones Especiales**?
4. How many times a year will you receive an **Edición Especial**?
5. How much does it cost (in pesos) to subscribe only to **México desconocido**?

16.10 WRITING EXERCISE

You have learned about Mexico in several lessons so far. Write a short description of eight to ten sentences about Mexico. Refer to the information in this lesson and in Lesson 8.

VOCABULARY

NOUNS

la comida	*food*	**el (la) músico**	*musician*
la enchilada	*enchilada (Mexican dish with tortillas, filling, and sauce)*	**el país**	*country, nation*
		la piscina	*pool*
		la quesadilla	*quesadilla (toasted tortilla with cheese)*
el entusiasmo	*enthusiasm*	**el taco**	*taco (tortilla filled with meat, fish, or vegetables)*
la gente	*people*		
el hombre	*man*		
la montaña	*mountain*	**el valle**	*valley*
la mujer	*woman*		

VERBS

bailar	*to dance*

ADJECTIVES

alto	*high, tall*
rico(a)	*tasty, rich*
romántico(a)	*romantic*

OTHER WORDS AND EXPRESSIONS

como	*such as*

LESSON 17

✺

En el aeropuerto
- The months of the year
- The past tense of the verb **ir**
- Traveling by airplane

17.1 THE AIRPORT

el mes pasado	*last month*	julio	*July*
el año pasado	*last year*	agosto	*August*
la semana pasada	*last week*	septiembre	*September*
		octubre	*October*
el lunes (martes, etc.) pasado	*last Monday (Tuesday, etc.)*	noviembre	*November*
		diciembre	*December*
hoy	*today*	en junio	*in June*
ayer	*yesterday*	el aeropuerto	*airport*
anoche	*last night*	Fui.	*I went.*
enero	*January*	No fui.	*I didn't go.*
febrero	*February*	Fue.	*You/He/She/It went.*
marzo	*March*	¿Fue usted?	*Did you go?*
abril	*April*	hacer	*to make, to do*
mayo	*May*	¿Qué va a hacer?	*What are you going to do?*
junio	*June*		

Spelling: Days of the week and months of the year

The months of the year and the days of the week are not written with a capital
letter in Spanish.

17.2 LISTENING EXERCISE

Repeat each sentence after your instructor says it, reading along in the book as
you speak.

1. Fui al cine anoche.
2. Fui al cine con Roberto.
3. Fui al parque esta tarde.
4. Fui a la clase esta tarde.
5. Fui al teatro anoche.
6. Fui al banco ayer.
7. Fui a nadar esta tarde.
8. Fui al cine después de la cena.
9. Fui al parque después de la clase.
10. No fui al cine anoche.
11. No fui al parque esta tarde.
12. Roberto fue al cine.
13. María fue al cine.
14. El doctor fue al hospital.
15. Roberto fue al cine después de la cena.
16. María no fue al cine anoche.
17. Roberto no fue al teatro anoche.
18. Fui a California en junio.

17.3 ORAL EXERCISE

Answer the following questions.

EXAMPLE: **¿Fue usted al cine anoche?**
ANSWER: **Sí, fui al cine anoche.**

1. ¿Fue usted al cine solo (sola)?
2. ¿Fue usted a una fiesta el sábado?
3. ¿Fue tu compañero(a) de cuarto a clase esta mañana?
4. ¿Fue usted a nadar después de las clases ayer?
5. ¿Fue tu amigo al cine después de las clases ayer?
6. ¿Fue usted al parque esta mañana?
7. ¿Fue usted al teatro el mes pasado?
8. ¿Fue tu amiga al aeropuerto el año pasado?
9. ¿Fue usted al banco la semana pasada?
10. ¿Fue usted a jugar baloncesto ayer?

Can you do this exercise with your book closed?

17.4 ORAL EXERCISE

Answer the following questions.

1. ¿Fue usted al cine anoche?
2. ¿Fue usted a una fiesta la semana pasada?
3. ¿Fue tu mamá al banco ayer?
4. ¿Fue usted a nadar esta semana?
5. ¿Fue usted a clase ayer?
6. ¿Va usted al cine mañana?
7. ¿Va usted a clase esta tarde?
8. ¿Va usted a la fiesta esta noche?
9. ¿Va usted a nadar mañana?
10. ¿Fue tu papá al aeropuerto el año pasado?
11. ¿Va usted a la estación este mes?
12. ¿Va el profesor (la profesora) al parque después de la clase?
13. ¿Fue usted al cine después de la cena?
14. ¿Fue el profesor (la profesora) a nadar después de la clase?
15. ¿Qué va a hacer usted después de la clase hoy?

Grammar: Using the verb **ir** in the past tense

The verb ir (to go) is a very irregular verb in Spanish. It stands on its own and must not be compared with other verbs since it doesn't follow the same rules. You already know the present tense forms of this verb.

Below are the present and past tenses of the verb ir. Review them so that you will remember them easily.

present tense of **ir**		past tense of **ir**	
voy	vamos	fui	fuimos
vas	vais	fuiste	fuisteis
va	van	fue	fueron

Fui.	*I went.*	**¿Fui?**	*Did I go?*
Fuiste.	*You went. (fam.)*	**¿Fuiste?**	*Did you go? (fam.)*
Fue.	*You went. (formal)*	**¿Fue?**	*Did you go? (formal)*
	He went.		*Did he go?*
	She went.		*Did she go?*
	It went.		*Did it go?*
Fuimos.	*We went.*	**¿Fuimos?**	*Did we go?*
Fueron.	*You went. (pl. formal)*	**¿Fueron?**	*Did you go? (pl. formal)*
	They went.		*Did they go?*

EXAMPLES: — ¿**Vas al cine?**　　*Are you going to the movies?*
　　　　　 — **No, fui ayer.**　　*No, I went yesterday.*

17.5 CONVERSATION VOCABULARY

el (la) maletero(a)	porter	Vaya a la sala de espera.	Go to the waiting room.
¿En qué vuelo?	On what flight?	el número	number
su equipaje	your luggage	Perdón, señor (señora, señorita).	Excuse me, sir (ma'am, miss).
esa valija/maleta	that suitcase		
Voy a facturarla.	I'm going to check it.	llega	arrive, arrives
Voy a llevarla.	I'm going to carry it.	el asiento	seat
el boleto/billete	ticket	¿Qué asiento tiene?	Where are you sitting? (What seat do you have?)
su pasaporte	your passport		
Escriba su nombre.	Write your name.		
Escríbalo en el formulario.	Write it on the form.	Pase por aquí.	Step this way.
		¿Tomamos el desayuno?	Shall we have breakfast?
su dirección	your address		
en una hora	in an hour	¿A qué hora?	At what time?
¿Sale el vuelo...?	Does the flight leave...?	Ajuste su cinturón.	Fasten your seatbelt.

¿Se permite fumar?	*Is smoking allowed?*	**Aquí está.**	*Here it is. Here he/she is.*
Despegar	*to take off*	**Aquí viene.**	*Here it comes. Here he/she comes.*
Aterrizar	*to land*		
Necesitar	*to need*	**Allí está.**	*There it is. There he/she is.*
Lo necesito.	*I need it.*		
Aquí hay uno.	*Here's one.*	**Allí viene.**	*There it comes. Here he/she comes.*
el auto	*car*		
el coche		**Allá está.**	*There (over there) it is. There (over there) he/she is.*
el carro			
la puerta	*door, gate*		
la aduana	*customs*	**Allá viene.**	*There (over there) it comes. There (over there) he/she comes.*
Aquí lo tiene.	*Here it is. (You have it.)*		
Lo tengo aquí.	*Here it is. (I have it.)*		

🔲 17.6 CONVERSATION

Your instructor will select students to take the roles of the airline agent and the traveler, the flight attendant and the traveler, or of the traveler's friends and the traveler.

The following block will serve as a guide for your conversation. However, do not restrict yourself only to what is in the block.

Check-in counter at the airport

AIRLINE AGENT: ¿Adónde va?

TRAVELER: A San Antonio.

AIRLINE AGENT: ¿En qué vuelo?

TRAVELER: En el vuelo trescientos.

AIRLINE AGENT: ¿Dónde está su equipaje?

TRAVELER:	Lo tengo aquí.
AIRLINE AGENT:	¿Y esa valija?
TRAVELER:	Voy a llevarla en la mano.
AIRLINE AGENT:	Su boleto, por favor.
TRAVELER:	Sí, señorita (señor). Aquí lo tiene.
AIRLINE AGENT:	Su pasaporte, por favor.
TRAVELER:	Aquí está.
AIRLINE AGENT:	Escriba su nombre y su dirección aquí, por favor.
TRAVELER:	¿A qué hora sale el vuelo trescientos?
AIRLINE AGENT:	A las ocho. Aquí tiene su boleto. Y su pasaporte. Vaya a la sala de espera número cinco.
TRAVELER:	Perdón, señorita (señor). ¿A qué hora llega el avión a San Antonio?
AIRLINE AGENT:	A las dos de la tarde.

On the airplane

FLIGHT ATTENDANT:	¿Qué asiento tiene?
TRAVELER:	El número diez.
FLIGHT ATTENDANT:	Pase por aquí, por favor. Aquí está.
TRAVELER:	Gracias, señorita (señor). ¿A qué hora tomamos el desayuno?
FLIGHT ATTENDANT:	En una hora. Ajuste su cinturón, por favor.
TRAVELER:	¿Se permite fumar?
FLIGHT ATTENDANT:	Después de despegar, señor (señorita).
TRAVELER:	¿A qué hora aterrizamos?
FLIGHT ATTENDANT:	A las dos de la tarde.

On arrival

FIRST FRIEND:	Mira, allí está Bernardo. ¡Bernardo!
SECOND FRIEND:	¿Dónde?
FIRST FRIEND:	Allí, enfrente de la aduana. ¡Bernardo!
SECOND FRIEND:	Allí viene. ¡Bernardo! ¿Cómo estás, amigo?
BERNARDO:	Bien, ¿y tú?
SECOND FRIEND:	Muy bien.
BERNARDO:	Necesito un maletero. Aquí hay uno. Por favor, señor.
FIRST FRIEND:	Bernardo, estamos muy contentos de verte.
BERNARDO:	Yo también.
FIRST FRIEND:	El coche está directamente enfrente de la puerta.
SECOND FRIEND:	Vamos a la casa.
BERNARDO:	¡Qué bueno!

17.7 READING EXERCISE: IBERIA, LA AEROLÍNEA ESPAÑOLA

In this lesson, you learned some new words and expressions to use when traveling by plane. See if you can put them to work in reading this advertisement for Iberia airlines. Use the list of new words provided to guide you as you read the advertisement and use your guessing skills to figure out other words that you don't know. Then answer the questions that follow.

agente de viajes	*travel agent*	**viajar**	*to travel*
		disfruta	*enjoy*
vuela	*flies*	**su equipaje de mano**	*carry-on luggage*
sin escala	*nonstop*		

IBERIA

¡Volamos por el mundo adonde todo el mundo quiere volar!

IBERIA PRESENTA SERVICIO «CABINA ANCHA» A MADRID 5 DÍAS A LA SEMANA.

Bienvenido a bordo del nuevo 747 de Iberia. El avión de «cabina ancha» más avanzado tecnológicamente ahora está volando sin escala 5 días a la semana a las 6:10 p.m. de San Juan a Madrid.

El 747 vuela suave y silenciosamente. La «cabina ancha» le ofrece más espacio para usted y su equipaje de mano. Y como siempre, usted disfruta del servicio y la hospitalidad que son tradicionales de Iberia...tanto en la lujosa primera clase como en la acogedora económica. Cuando usted quiera viajar a Madrid, o a cualquier ciudad de España, llame a su agente de viajes para que le reserve un asiento en el fabuloso 747 de Iberia.

1. What do you think **cabina ancha** means?

2. How many weekly nonstop flights are there to Madrid from San Juan?

3. What does **el nuevo 747 de Iberia** offer?
4. What will you enjoy when you travel with Iberia?
5. Whom should you call to reserve a seat?

17.8 WRITING EXERCISE

When you travel, what do you have in your suitcase? How many suitcases do you bring? When do you like to travel? Do you travel by plane? If so, what kind of seat do you get? Write a short description of your typical travel plans. Write six to eight complete Spanish sentences, using the vocabulary from this and previous lessons.

VOCABULARY

NOUNS

abril	*April*	julio	*July*
la aduana	*customs*	junio	*June*
el aeropuerto	*airport*	el lunes (martes,	*last Monday*
agosto	*August*	etc.) pasado	*(Tuesday, etc.)*
anoche	*last night*	el (la) maletero(a)	*porter*
el año pasado	*last year*	la maleta	*suitcase*
el asiento	*seat*	marzo	*March*
el auto	*car*	mayo	*May*
ayer	*yesterday*	el mes pasado	*last month*
el billete	*ticket*	el nombre	*name*
el boleto	*ticket*	noviembre	*November*
el carro	*car*	el número	*number*
el cinturón	*belt, seatbelt*	octubre	*October*
el coche	*car*	el pasaporte	*passport*
diciembre	*December*	la puerta	*door, gate*
la dirección	*address*	la sala de espera	*waiting room*
enero	*January*	la semana pasada	*last week*
el equipaje	*luggage*	septiembre	*September*
febrero	*February*	la valija	*suitcase*
hoy	*today*	el vuelo	*flight*

VERBS

ajustar	*to adjust*	hacer	*to make, to do*
aterrizar	*to land*	llegar	*to arrive*
despegar	*to take off*	necesitar	*to need*

OTHER WORDS AND EXPRESSIONS

Ajuste su cinturón.	*Fasten your seatbelt.*	¿Fue usted?	*Did you go?*
Allá está.	*Over there it/he/she is.*	Lo necesito.	*I need it.*
		Lo tengo aquí.	*Here it is. (I have it.)*
Allá viene.	*Over there it/he/she comes.*	Pase por aquí.	*Step this way.*
		Perdón, señor (señora, señorita).	*Pardon me, sir (ma'am, miss).*
Allí está.	*There it/he/she is.*		
Allí viene.	*There it he/she comes.*	¿Qué asiento tiene?	*What seat do you have?*
Aquí está.	*Here it/he/she is.*		
Aquí hay uno.	*Here's one.*	¿Qué va a hacer?	*What are you going to do?*
Aquí lo tiene.	*Here it is. (You have it.)*		
		¿Sale el vuelo...?	*Does the flight leave...*
Aquí viene.	*Here it/he/she comes.*	¿Se permite fumar?	*Is smoking allowed?*
¿En qué vuelo?	*On what flight?*		
en una hora	*in an hour*	Vaya a la sala de espera.	*Go to the waiting room.*
Escriba su nombre.	*Write your name.*		
		Voy a facturarla.	*I'm going to check it.*
Escríbalo en el formulario.	*Write it on the form.*	Voy a llevarla.	*I'm going to carry it.*

LESSON 18

Los pasatiempos

- The past tense (preterite) of **-ar** verbs, singular forms
- The personal **a**
- **Llevar** and **tomar**
- Talking about weekend activities

Grammar: Forming the past tense of singular -ar verbs

To form the singular past tense forms of regular -ar verbs, remove the -ar from the infinitive and add these endings: -é, -aste, -ó.

cocinar	*to cook*	limpiar	*to clean*
cociné	*I cooked*	limpié	*I cleaned*
cocinaste	*you cooked (fam.)*	limpiaste	*you cleaned (fam.)*
cocinó	*you/he/she cooked*	limpió	*you/he/she cleaned*
comprar	*to buy*	nadar	*to swim*
compré	*I bought*	nadé	*I swam*
compraste	*you bought (fam.)*	nadaste	*you swam (fam.)*
compró	*you/he/she bought*	nadó	*you/he/she swam*
pintar	*to paint*	contestar	*to answer*
pinté	*I painted*	contesté	*I answered*
pintaste	*you painted (fam.)*	contestaste	*you answered (fam.)*
pintó	*you/he/she painted*	contestó	*you/he/she answered*
ganar	*to win, to earn*	alquilar	*to rent*
gané	*I won, earned*	alquilé	*I rented*
ganaste	*you won, earned (fam.)*	alquilaste	*you rented (fam.)*
ganó	*you/he/she won, earned*	alquiló	*you/he/she rented*
ayudar	*to help, to aid*	llevar	*to take*
ayudé	*I helped*	llevé	*I took*
ayudaste	*you helped (fam.)*	llevaste	*you took (fam.)*
ayudó	*you/he/she helped*	llevó	*you/he/she took*

caminar	to walk	pasar	to spend (time, a vacation)
caminé	I walked	pasé	I spent
caminaste	you walked (fam.)	pasaste	you spent (fam.)
caminó	you/he/she walked	pasó	you/he/she spent
estacionar	to park (car)	llamar	to call
estacioné	I parked	llamé	I called
estacionaste	you parked (fam.)	llamaste	you called (fam.)
estacionó	you/he/she parked	llamó	you/he/she called

EXAMPLES:

Ayer, caminé dos millas.　　　*Yesterday I walked two miles.*
Mi mamá pintó la casa.　　　*My mother painted the house.*
¿Limpiaste la casa?　　　*Did you clean the house?*

18.1 RECREATIONAL ACTIVITIES

la lancha	boat	mi abuela	my grandmother
la lancha de motor	motor boat	la sala	living room
		el cuarto	room
el baño	bathroom, bath	Mi tía contestó el teléfono.	My aunt answered the phone.
la cocina	kitchen, cuisine		
el (la) cocinero(a)	cook, chef	¿Qué hiciste?	What did you do? (fam.)
la cabaña	cabin, cabana	¿Qué hiciste este fin de semana?	What did you do this weekend? (fam.)
el (la) pintor(a)	painter		
el baño de sol	sun bath	¿Qué hizo usted?	What did you do?
conmigo	with me	¿Qué hizo usted este fin de semana?	What did you do this weekend?
Me ayudó.	He/She/It helped me.		
mi abuelo	my grandfather		

🔲 18.2 LISTENING EXERCISE

Repeat each sentence after your instructor says it, reading along in the book as you speak.

1. Roberto compró una lancha.
2. Bárbara pintó la lancha.
3. Fuimos a la cabaña.
4. Roberto limpió el baño.
5. Bárbara limpió la cocina.
6. Bernardo contestó el teléfono.
7. Bernardo alquiló una lancha.
8. Yo pinté la lancha.
9. Bernardo alquiló una cabaña en la playa.
10. María alquiló una lancha de motor.
11. Mi tío Luis alquiló una casa.
12. Bernardo limpió la casa.

18.3 ORAL EXERCISE

Answer the following questions.

1. ¿Qué hizo usted este fin de semana?
2. ¿Alquiló usted una lancha de motor?
3. ¿Pintó usted la casa?
4. ¿Caminó usted en la playa?
5. ¿Limpió usted la casa?
6. ¿Pasó usted unos días en las montañas?
7. ¿Quién cocinó la cena anoche?
8. ¿Habló usted por teléfono esta mañana?
9. ¿Quién contestó el teléfono cuando usted llamó?
10. ¿Tomó usted un baño de sol este fin de semana?
11. ¿Fue usted al cine?
12. ¿Fueron usted y sus amigos a una fiesta?

Can you do this exercise with your book closed?

18.4 ORAL OR WRITTEN EXERCISE

Create sentences in the past tense using the cues provided.

EXAMPLE: (contestar) María ... el teléfono.
ANSWER: María contestó el teléfono.

1. (comprar)   María ... tomates en el supermercado.
2. (alquilar)   Bernardo ... una casa muy bonita.
3. (pintar)   María ... la lancha de motor.
4. (hablar)   Yo ... con mi tío esta mañana.
5. (limpiar)   Yo ... la casa esta mañana.
6. (ayudar)   María me ...
7. (comprar)   Bárbara ... una bicicleta.
8. (tomar)   Susana ... una taza de café.
9. (pintar)   Yo ... la cocina.
10. (ganar)   Bernardo ... esta tarde.
11. (trabajar)   Mi tío ... el sábado.
12. (nadar)   Mi abuelo ... esta mañana.
13. (bailar)   Mi tío ... con mi tía.
14. (nadar)   Yo ... esta mañana.
15. (llevar)   María ... el libro a la clase.
16. (cocinar)   Roberto ... en la cocina.

18.5 COMPOSITION VOCABULARY

toda la mañana	*the whole morning*	**Todos hablamos.**	*We all talked (spoke).*
con nosotros	*with us*	**Me llevó.**	*He/She took me.*
Tomamos...	*We had...*	**Hizo...**	*He/She made...*
nuestros amigos	*our friends*	**el dulce**	*candy*
La compró.	*He/She bought it.*	**la limonada**	*lemonade*

18.6 LISTENING EXERCISE

Listen to the following composition as your instructor reads it aloud. Read along in your book, paying particular attention to the pronunciation of the Spanish words.

El fin de semana

El sábado fui a visitar a mi amigo Carlos. Fui a su casa en auto. La casa de Carlos está en la playa. ¡Es muy bonita! Pasé el fin de semana en su casa. Nadé con Carlos toda la mañana. María fue a la playa también y nadó con nosotros. En la playa tomamos limonada, sándwiches, una ensalada y dulces. Carlos hizo unos sándwiches deliciosos. María hizo la ensalada.

El domingo, Carlos me llevó a una fiesta en la casa de unos amigos. Roberto tocó la guitarra muy bien. Tiene una guitarra muy bonita. La compró en Caracas. María cantó canciones mexicanas. Canta muy bien. Todos hablamos español con nuestros amigos. Son muy simpáticos.

18.7 ORAL EXERCISE

Read each sentence in the composition above and translate it into English.

18.8 READING EXERCISE

Now read aloud a whole paragraph of the composition. Try to read as smoothly as you can.

Grammar: The personal a

In Spanish, you use an **a** after a verb when it is followed by a person. This **a**, which goes between the verb and the person, is known as the personal **a**.

EXAMPLES:

Invité a Carlos.	*I invited Carlos.*
Visité a Marta.	*I visited Marta.*
Llevé a Marta al cine.	*I took Marta to the movies.*

This personal **a** has no equivalent in English.

When a personal **a** comes before the article **el**, you use the contraction **al.**

a + el = al

EXAMPLES:

El doctor curó al paciente.	*The doctor cured the patient.*
El doctor examinó al paciente.	*The doctor examined the patient.*
Recomendé al doctor.	*I recommended the doctor.*
Llevé al doctor a mi casa.	*I took the doctor to my house.*

This structure is used in all tenses.

FUTURE:

Voy a visitar a Juan.	*I'm going to visit Juan.*
Susana va a invitar a Roberto.	*Susana is going to invite Roberto.*

PRESENT:

El doctor examina a los pacientes.	*The doctor examines the patients.*
Invito a Roberto a todas las fiestas.	*I invite Roberto to all the parties.*

PAST:

Mi tía llamó a mis abuelos.	*My aunt called my grandparents.*
Visité a mi abuelo.	*I visited my grandfather.*

When you talk about pets, use the personal **a** as if the pet were a person.

Llevé a Napoleón, mi perro, al parque.	*I took Napoleón, my dog, to the park.*

18.9 ORAL OR WRITTEN EXERCISE

For each sentence, insert a personal **a** only where it is needed. Remember to use the personal **a** only when a person follows the verb.

EXAMPLE: **Visité … Pedro en el hospital.**
ANSWER: **Visité a Pedro en el hospital.**
EXAMPLE: **Visité … la Casa Blanca en Washington.**
ANSWER: **Visité la Casa Blanca en Washington.**

1. Llevé … Roberto a la playa.

2. Invité … Bernardo a la fiesta.

3. Llevé … el libro a la clase.

4. Llevé … el radio a la playa.

5. Llevé … mi tío a la estación.

6. Llamé … la profesora por teléfono.

7. Estacioné … el auto.

8. Ayudé … mi mamá con el trabajo.

9. Ayudé … con el trabajo.

10. Contesté … el teléfono.

Grammar: How to use **llevar** and **tomar**

Llevar means *to take* in the sense of taking someone or something somewhere. **Tomar** means *to take* in most other senses, such as to take a taxi, to take a lesson, or to take a drink.

EXAMPLES:

Llevé a María a la estación.	*I took María to the station.*
Roberto llevó a Susana a una fiesta.	*Roberto took Susana to a party.*
Llevamos los sándwiches a la playa.	*We took the sandwiches to the beach.*
Tomé un taxi.	*I took a taxi.*
En esa escuela, toman clases de español.	*At that school, they take Spanish lessons.*
En la playa tomamos limonada y jugo de naranja.	*We bad (took) lemonade and orange juice at the beach.*

18.10 ORAL OR WRITTEN EXERCISE

Use the columns of words provided to create sentences.

I	II	III
Compré	tomates	en el supermercado
Compraste	bistec	en la tienda
Compró	rosbif	en la tienda de música
Mi amigo(a) compró	un sombrero	en la playa
	un suéter	
	una blusa	
	pantalones	
	un radio	
	discos compactos	
	un sándwich	
	una camisa	
	guantes	
	zapatos	
	chicle	
	chocolates	
	limonada	

I	II	III
Llevé	sándwiches	a la playa
Llevaste	limonada	a la cabaña
Llevó	una ensalada	a la casa
Mi compañero(a)	la lancha	al apartamento
de cuarto llevó	el libro	a la estación
	dulces	a la clase
	frutas	a la escuela
	el radio	a la oficina
	discos compactos	al hotel
	a (name)	al parque
	a (name)	al hospital
	al doctor	a la fiesta
	al perro	
	al niño *(the boy)*	
	a la niña *(the girl)*	

18.11 CONVERSATION VOCABULARY

Ganaron Los Tigres. *The Tigers won.*

Estudié una sonata de violín. *I studied a violin sonata.*

Vimos una comedia muy chistosa. *We saw a very funny comedy.*

toda la tarde *all afternoon*

chistoso(a) *funny*

béisbol *baseball*

¿Te fuiste a nadar el domingo? *Did you go swimming (to swim) on Sunday?*

18.12 CONVERSATION

Form groups of two students and conduct a conversation about a weekend at home. The following block will serve as a guide for your conversation. However, do not restrict yourself only to what is in the block.

A weekend at home

FIRST STUDENT: ¿Dónde pasaste el fin de semana?

SECOND STUDENT: En casa.

FIRST STUDENT: ¿Estudiaste mucho?

SECOND STUDENT: Sí, estudié mucho. Estudié mi libro de español. También estudié música. Estudié una sonata de violín (de piano).

FIRST STUDENT:	¿Trabajaste en el jardín?
SECOND STUDENT:	Sí, trabajé toda la tarde en el jardín.
FIRST STUDENT:	¿Fuiste al cine el sábado?
SECOND STUDENT:	Sí. Llevé a María al cine y vimos una comedia muy chistosa.
FIRST STUDENT:	¿Fuiste al fútbol el domingo?
SECOND STUDENT:	Sí, fui al fútbol con Carlos.
FIRST STUDENT:	¿Quién ganó?
SECOND STUDENT:	Ganaron Los Metropolitanos.
FIRST STUDENT:	¡Ah, caramba! ¿Tú fuiste al béisbol?
SECOND STUDENT:	Sí. Fui al béisbol con Roberto.
FIRST STUDENT:	¿Quién ganó?
SECOND STUDENT:	Ganaron Los Tigres.
FIRST STUDENT:	¡Qué bueno!

18.13 READING EXERCISE: LA VIDA EN VIDEO 8

In this lesson, you learned to talk about what you did over the weekend. The advertisement on the opposite page is for a product that not only allows people to talk about what they did, but to show it as well. Read the advertisement with the help of the words provided, then complete the exercise that follows.

la vida	*life*
el deporte	*sports*
grabar	*to tape, to record*
hasta	*up to*
alta calidad	*high quality*

1. See if you can list in English the five different categories of activities that the ad says you can videotape.

2. What clues helped you figure out the categories you didn't recognize at first?

3. How many uninterrupted hours of tape can you record with this camera?

4. What other things can you do with it? (List at least three.)

5. What can you do with your television set and the camera?

18.14 WRITING EXERCISE

Imagine you have a day free to do whatever you want to do. How would you spend your time? Write six to eight complete sentences in Spanish describing your activities, who you would do them with, at what time, and where.

VOCABULARY

NOUNS

la abuela	*grandmother*	el dulce	*candy*
el abuelo	*grandfather*	la lancha	*boat*
el baño	*bathroom, bath*	la lancha de	*motor boat*
el baño de sol	*sun bath*	motor	
	(sunbathing)	la limonada	*lemonade*
el béisbol	*baseball*	la niña	*girl*
la cabaña	*cabin, cabana*	el niño	*boy*
la cocina	*kitchen, cuisine*	el (la) pintor(a)	*painter*
el (la) cocinero(a)	*cook, chef*	la sala	*living room*
la comedia	*comedy*	la sonata de	*violin sonata*
el cuarto	*room*	violín	

VERBS

alquilar	*to rent*	ganar	*to win, to earn*
ayudar	*to help*	limpiar	*to clean*
caminar	*to walk*	llamar	*to call*
cocinar	*to cook*	llevar	*to take*
contestar	*to answer*	pasar	*to spend (time)*
estacionar	*to park*	pintar	*to paint*

ADJECTIVES

chistoso(a)	*funny*

OTHER WORDS AND EXPRESSIONS

conmigo	*with me*	¿Qué hizo usted?	*What did you do?*
con nosotros	*with us*	¿Qué hizo usted	*What did you do*
Ganaron.	*You (pl. formal)/*	este fin de	*this weekend?*
	They won, earned.	semana?	
Hizo…	*He/she made…*	¿Te fuiste a nadar	*Did you go swim-*
nuestro(a)	*our*	el domingo?	*ming on Sunday?*
La compró.	*He/She bought it.*	toda la mañana	*all morning*
Me ayudó.	*He/She/It helped me.*	Todos hablamos.	*We all talked.*
Me llevó.	*He/She took me.*	Tomamos…	*We had.*
¿Qué hiciste?	*What did you do?*	Vimos…	*We saw…*
	(fam.)		
¿Qué hiciste	*What did you do*		
este fin de	*this weekend? (fam.)*		
semana?			

LESSON 19

✳

Las vacaciones
- The past tense (preterite) of all regular **-ar** verbs
- **Jugar, estar, tener,** and **andar** in the past
- The seasons of the year
- Talking about vacations

Grammar: The past tense of all regular **-ar** verbs

The *we* form of **-ar** verbs is identical in the present and in the past tenses.
Remove the **-ar** and add **-amos**. To form the third person plural, remove the **-ar**
and add **-aron**.

EXAMPLES:

comprar	to buy	hablar	to speak
compramos	we bought	hablamos	we spoke
compraron	you bought (pl.), they bought	hablaron	you spoke (pl.), they spoke
llevar	to take	trabajar	to work
llevamos	we took	trabajamos	we worked
llevaron	you took (pl.), they took	trabajaron	you worked (pl.), they worked
estudiar	to study	nadar	to swim
estudiamos	we studied	nadamos	we swam
estudiaron	you studied (pl.), they studied	nadaron	you swam (pl.), they swam
terminar	to finish	contestar	to answer
terminamos	we finished	contestamos	we answered
terminaron	you finished (pl.), they finished	contestaron	you answered (pl.), they answered
caminar	to walk	regresar	to return, to get back
caminamos	we walked	regresamos	we returned, we got back
caminaron	you walked (pl.), they walked	regresaron	you returned, you got back (pl.), they returned, they got back

EXAMPLES:	**Terminamos el trabajo y caminamos por el parque.**	*We finished the work and walked through the park.*
	Compraron cinco libros y llevaron tres a casa.	*They bought five books and they brought three home.*

Notes: Regresar means *to return, to get back, to come back.*

EXAMPLE:	**Regresamos del campo.**	*We returned (got back, came back) from the country.*

Remember that the they form and the you (pl. formal) forms are identical. Each of the above **-aron** verb forms has four English translations.

EXAMPLE:	**Compraron...**	*You bought... (pl. formal)*
		Did you buy...? (pl. formal)
		They bought...
		Did they buy...?

19.1 ENJOYING THE COUNTRYSIDE

el club	*club*	los naipes	*playing cards*
el bridge	*bridge (the card game)*	el videojuego	*videogame*
el campo	*countryside*	el golf	*golf*
yo	*I*	el bosque	*forest*
y yo	*and I*	el árbol	*tree*
nosotros	*we*	el río	*river*
el lago	*lake*		

19.2 LISTENING EXERCISE

Repeat each sentence after your instructor says it, reading along in the book as you speak. Stress the word **yo** firmly.

1. Roberto y yo compramos dulces.
2. Roberto y yo jugamos videojuegos.
3. Luis y yo estudiamos la lección.
4. María y yo tomamos café en un restaurante.
5. Luis y yo preparamos la lección muy bien.
6. Roberto y yo nadamos en un lago muy lindo el sábado.
7. Mamá y yo caminamos en el bosque el domingo.
8. Mamá y yo llevamos a María al cine.
9. Papá y yo llevamos a Roberto al campo.
10. María y yo hablamos en español en la clase.
11. Mi mamá y yo regresamos a la casa tarde.
12. Roberto y Luis jugaron tenis.
13. Roberto y María jugaron bridge anoche con mamá y papá.
14. Roberto y Luis jugaron golf en el club el sábado.
15. Luis y María cantaron canciones mexicanas anoche.
16. Cantaron muy bien.
17. Hablaron muy bien.
18. Nadaron en el río.
19. Jugaron videojuegos muy bien.
20. Roberto y María visitaron a Luis el sábado.
21. Roberto y Carmen invitaron a Luis a la fiesta.

19.3 ORAL EXERCISE

Answer the following questions.

1. ¿En qué actividades participaron usted y sus amigos este fin de semana?
2. ¿Llevaron a sus abuelos al campo?
3. ¿Jugaron golf?
4. ¿Nadaron?
5. ¿Jugaron tenis en el campo?
6. ¿Fueron a la playa?
7. ¿Jugaron bridge?
8. ¿Compraron videojuegos?
9. ¿Estudiaron mucho?
10. ¿Regresaron tarde a casa?

19.4 ORAL OR WRITTEN EXERCISE

Give the **we** and **they** forms (past tense) of the following verbs.

EXAMPLE: **comprar**
ANSWER: **compramos, compraron**

1. llevar
2. invitar
3. hablar
4. cantar
5. alquilar
6. bailar
7. regresar
8. votar
9. visitar
10. jugar
11. recomendar
12. terminar
13. tomar
14. preparar
15. caminar
16. estudiar
17. nadar
18. notar
19. llevar
20. trabajar

19.5 ORAL EXERCISE

Answer the following questions.

1. ¿Qué hizo usted anoche?
2. ¿Fueron ustedes al cine?
3. ¿Invitó a su compañero(a) de cuarto a un restaurante?
4. ¿Jugó al baloncesto?

5. ¿Compró flores en el mercado?

6. ¿Fue a una fiesta?

7. ¿Qué hicieron usted y sus amigos la semana pasada?

8. ¿Nadaron en un lago o en una piscina?

9. ¿Tomaron la cena en un restaurante?

10. ¿Llevaron a su familia al campo?

11. ¿Invitaron a otros amigos a una fiesta?

12. ¿Regresaron tarde?

Grammar: The past tense of all regular -ar verbs (summary)

To form the past tense of all regular -ar verbs, remove the -ar from the infinitive, and add the following endings:

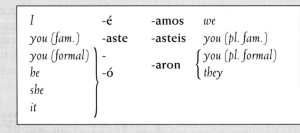

I	-é	-amos	*we*
you (fam.)	-aste	-asteis	*you (pl. fam.)*
you (formal)	-	-aron	*you (pl. formal)*
he	-ó		*they*
she			
it			

The great majority of verbs in Spanish are regular -ar verbs. Therefore, if you learn this chart, you will know how to form the past tense of many Spanish verbs.

19.6 ORAL OR WRITTEN EXERCISE

There are hundreds of -ar verbs that are similar in English and Spanish. Try using some of these verbs in this exercise.

For each infinitive, give the corresponding form of the verb in the past tense.

EXAMPLE: **Yo/marchar**   *to march*
ANSWER: **Yo marché**.

1.	**tú/invitar**	*to invite*	6.	**tú procesar**	*to process*
2.	**nosotros/visitar**	*to visit*	7.	**ella depositar**	*to deposit*
3.	**Yo/plantar**	*to plant*	8.	**Tú y yo protestar**	*to protest*
4.	**Uds./dictar**	*to dictate*	9.	**Ud./inventar**	*to invent*
5.	**ellos/recomendar**	*to recommend*	10.	**Yo/entrar**	*to enter, to go in, to come in*

Can you do this exercise with your book closed?

19.7 REVIEW—MINI-TEST

Now that you know how to form the past tense of any regular -**ar** verb in the Spanish language, give the five forms of the past tense of the following new verbs. You have never seen these verbs before, but you can form the past tense easily because they are regular -**ar** verbs.

1.	**formar**	*to form*	6.	**grabar**	*to tape, to record*
2.	**lavar**	*to wash*	7.	**escapar**	*to escape*
3.	**mandar**	*to send*	8.	**planchar**	*to iron (clothes)*
4.	**saltar**	*to jump*	9.	**esperar**	*to wait, to hope*
5.	**reservar**	*to reserve*	10.	**levantar**	*to lift*

Grammar: Some high-frequency stem-changing verbs in the past tense

Some of the verbs that you use frequently are not regular in the preterite. Here are the preterite forms for some of these verbs.

jugar *to play (a game)*			
I played	**jugué**	**jugamos**	*we played*
you played (fam.)	**jugaste**	**jugasteis**	*you played (pl. fam.)*
you played (formal)			*you played (pl. formal)*
he played	**jugó**	**jugaron**	*they played*
she played			

Note: You insert a letter **u** before the e of the **yo** form of **jugar**. Otherwise it is a regular -**ar** verb.

Here are three verbs that share the same preterite forms.

tener *to have*

I had	**tuve**	**tuvimos**	*we had*
you had (fam.)	**tuviste**	**tuvisteis**	*you had (pl. fam.)*
you had (formal)			*you had (pl. formal)*
he had	**tuvo**	**tuvieron**	*they had*
she had			
it had			

andar *to walk, ride*

I walked, rode	**anduve**	**anduvimos**	*we walked, rode*
you walked, rode (fam.)	**anduviste**	**anduvisteis**	*you walked, rode (pl. fam.)*
you walked, rode (formal)			*you walked, rode (pl. formal)*
he walked, rode	**anduvo**	**anduvieron**	*they walked, rode*
she walked, rode			
it walked, rode			

estar *to be*

I was	**estuve**	**estuvimos**	*we were*
you were (fam.)	**estuviste**	**estuvisteis**	*you were (pl. fam.)*
you were (formal)			*you were (pl. formal)*
he was	**estuvo**	**estuvieron**	*they were*
she was			
it was			

Note: Notice that in **tener**, **andar**, and **estar**, the entire verb changes, not just the endings.

EXAMPLES:

Anduvimos hasta el parque y jugamos tenis.   *We walked to the park and we played tennis.*

Tuve un examen y estuve nervioso.   *I had a test and I was nervous.*

19.8 CONVERSATION VOCABULARY

el invierno   *winter*

la primavera   *spring*

el verano   *summer*

el otoño   *autumn*

todavía	*still*	**con él**	*with him*
la gatita	*kitten*	**Me invitó.**	*You/He/She invited me.*
el resto de	*the rest of*	**cuidar**	*to take care of*
cómodo(a)	*comfortable*	**Anduvimos**	*We rode bicycles.*
las vacaciones	*vacation*	**en bicicleta.**	
con ella	*with her*	**¿Tiene refri-**	*Does it have a*
		gerador?	*refrigerator?*

🔊 19.9 CONVERSATION

Form groups of two students and conduct a conversation about a vacation.

The following block will serve as a guide for your conversation. However, do not restrict yourself only to what is in the block.

A vacation

FIRST STUDENT: ¿Dónde pasaste tus vacaciones de verano?

SECOND STUDENT: En la playa.

FIRST STUDENT: ¿Fuiste a un hotel?

SECOND STUDENT: No, mi tío alquiló una cabaña en la playa y me invitó a pasar mis vacaciones con él.

FIRST STUDENT: ¿Invitó a (name) también?

SECOND STUDENT: Sí, invitó a (name) y a (name).

FIRST STUDENT: ¿Quién limpió la casa?

SECOND STUDENT: Yo limpié el baño, María limpió la cocina, y Bernardo y Bárbara limpiaron el resto de la cabaña.

FIRST STUDENT: ¿Quién cuidó el jardín?

SECOND STUDENT: Roberto cuidó el jardín y también limpió la terraza.

FIRST STUDENT: ¿Quién cocinó?

SECOND STUDENT: Todos cocinamos, pero Bernardo cocinó mucho. Es un cocinero fantástico.

FIRST STUDENT: ¿Anduvieron en bicicleta?

SECOND STUDENT: Sí, todos anduvimos en bicicleta. También anduvimos en lancha. Mi tío tiene una lancha chiquita. Y Bárbara alquiló una lancha de motor.

FIRST STUDENT: ¿Llevaste tu perro a la cabaña?

SECOND STUDENT: Sí, llevé a mi perro Napoleón y a mi gatita Cleopatra a la cabaña. Estuvieron muy contentos. Todos estuvimos muy contentos. La playa es muy linda.

FIRST STUDENT: ¿Es cómoda la cabaña?

SECOND STUDENT: Sí, muy cómoda.

FIRST STUDENT: ¿Tiene refrigerador?

SECOND STUDENT: Sí, tiene refrigerador, tostador eléctrico, televisor, teléfono y un radio.

FIRST STUDENT: ¿Cuando regresaste?

SECOND STUDENT: El veinte de agosto.

FIRST STUDENT: ¿Y adónde van a pasar las vacaciones de primavera?

SECOND STUDENT: ¡No sé todavía!

19.10 READING EXERCISE: CRUCEROS DE MIAMI

In this lesson, you learned about activities and ways that people spend their vacations. The following advertisement offers one way to plan an exciting vacation. Read the advertisement, with the help of the words provided, then complete the exercise that follows.

CRUCEROS DE MIAMI

El Nordic Empress, de RCCL, es el buque más lujoso entre los cruceros de 3 y 4 días, Miami — Bahamas.
Cruceros comenzando en octubre 1990

AMERICANA
(88 pasajeros)
Ivaran Line (buque de carga/crucero)
3 oct., 28 nov., 13 enero, 28 feb., 15 abril
46 noches
Rio de Janeiro, Santos, Buenos Aires,
Montevideo, Rio Grande du Sol, Itajai, Santos,
Rio de Janeiro, Salvador, Fortaleza, Norfolk,
Baltimore
También cruceros por segmentos
$7,590-$12,650
Tel. (305) 371-8714 (Miami)

NORDIC EMPRESS
Royal Caribbean Cruise Line
(1,610 pasajeros)
Los lunes hasta 25 marzo
4 noches — Nassau, Cococay, Freeport
$515-$1,245
Hasta 29 abril $525-$1,495
Los viernes hasta 29 marzo
3 noches — Nassau, Cococay $395-1,095
Hasta 26 abril $395-1,345
Tel: (305) 379-4731 y 1-800-327-6700 (E.U.A.)

DOLPHIN IV
Dolphin Cruises
(586 pasajeros)
Los viernes — 3 noches
Nassau, Blue Lagoon Island – $205-$525
Los lunes — 4 noches
Key West, Nassau, Blue Lagoon Island
$285-$655
Tel. (305) 358-2111 (Miami)

FANTASY
Carnival Cruise Lines
(2600 pasajeros)
Los viernes
3 noches — Nassau $345-$895
Los lunes
4 noches — Freeport, Nassau – $445-$1,035

HOLIDAY
Carnival Cruise Lines
(1,760 pasajeros)
Los sábados — 7 noches
Playa del Carmen, Cozumel, Gran Caimán,
Ocho Ríos – $795-$2,195

| el buque | *the ship* | lujoso(a) | *luxurious* |
| el crucero | *the cruise* | el (la) pasajero(a) | *the passenger* |

Now match the ship/cruise on the right with the desired situation on the left. Sometimes more than one ship or cruise may apply.

1. You're looking for the longest cruise available.
2. You want to travel on the smallest ship available.
3. You want to travel on the largest ship available.
4. You have less than $1000 to spend.
5. You want to go to South America.
6. You want to go to Blue Lagoon Island.
7. You want to go to Cococay.
8. You want to go to Cozumel.

a. Americana
b. Dolphin IV
c. Fantasy
d. Holiday
e. Nordic Empress

19.11 WRITING ACTIVITY

Describe a memorable vacation, answering the following questions. Write six to eight complete Spanish sentences.

1. ¿Adónde fue usted y cuándo?
2. ¿Qué hizo?
3. ¿Cuánto dinero gastó (*did you spend*)?
4. ¿En que estación del año fue usted?
5. ¿Con quién o con quiénes viajó?

VOCABULARY

NOUNS

el árbol	*tree*	los naipes	*playing cards*
el bosque	*forest*	el otoño	*autumn*
el bridge	*bridge (the card game)*	la primavera	*spring*
el campo	*countryside*	el refrigerador	*refrigerator*
el club	*club*	el resto	*rest*
la gatita	*kitten*	el río	*river*
el golf	*golf*	las vacaciones	*vacation*
el invierno	*winter*	el verano	*summer*
el lago	*lake*	el videojuego	*videogame*

VERBS

andar	*to walk to ride*	**regresar**	*to return, to get back*
cuidar	*to take care of*	**terminar**	*to finish*

ADJECTIVES

cómodo(a) *comfortable*

OTHER WORDS AND EXPRESSIONS

Anduvimos en bicicleta.	We rode bicycles.	**Me invitó.**	You/He/She invited me.
con él	with him	**nosotros**	we, us
con ella	with her	**todavía**	still

OPTIONAL LIST

VERBS

depositar	*to deposit*	**marchar**	*to march*
dictar	*to dictate*	**mandar**	*to send*
entrar	*to enter, to go in, to come in*	**planchar**	*to iron*
escapar	*to escape*	**plantar**	*to plant*
esperar	*to wait, to hope*	**procesar**	*to process*
formar	*to form*	**protestar**	*to protest*
grabar	*to tape, to record*	**recomendar**	*to recommend*
inventar	*to invent*	**reservar**	*to reserve*
invitar	*to invite*	**saltar**	*to jump*
lavar	*to wash*	**visitar**	*to visit*
levantar	*to lift*		

LESSON 20

❋

La vida diaria

- The past tense (preterite) of **leer**
- The past tense (preterite) of all regular **-er** and **-ir** verbs
- Using direct object pronouns
- Describing symptoms and illnesses

Grammar: Forming the singular past tense of **-er** and **-ir** verbs

To form the singular past tense of the -er and -ir verbs, remove the -er or -ir from the infinitive and add the following forms: -í, -iste, -ió.

EXAMPLES:

escribir	*to write*	comprender	*to understand*
escribí	*I wrote*	comprendí	*I understood*
escribiste	*you wrote (fam.)*	comprendiste	*you understood (fam.)*
escribió	*you/ he/ she wrote*	comprendió	*you/ he/ she understood*
decidir	*to decide*	ver	*to see*
decidí	*I decided*	vi	*I saw*
decidiste	*you decided (fam.)*	viste	*you saw (fam.)*
decidió	*you/ he/ she decided*	vio	*you/ he/ she saw*
recibir	*to receive*	vivir	*to live*
recibí	*I received*	viví	*I lived*
recibiste	*you received (fam.)*	viviste	*you lived (fam.)*
recibió	*you/ he/ she received*	vivió	*you/ he/ she lived*
vender	*to sell*	insistir	*to insist*
vendí	*I sold*	insistí	*I insisted*
vendiste	*you sold (fam.)*	insististe	*you insisted (fam.)*
vendió	*you/ he/ she sold*	insistió	*you/ he/ she insisted*

salir	to go out	comer	to eat
salí	I went out	comí	I ate
saliste	you went out (fam.)	comiste	you ate (fam.)
salió	you/ he/ she went out	comió	you/ he/ she ate

nacer	to be born
nací	I was born
naciste	you were born (fam.)
nació	you were born/ he/ she was born

EXAMPLES:

— ¿Decidiste ir a la fiesta?   *Did you decide to go to the party?*

— Sí, decidí que voy a ir.   *Yes, I decided I'm going to go. Susana decided to go*
   Susana decidió ir conmigo.   *with me.*

Another -er verb that you know, **leer**, is regular except in the third person. The y and accent marks are added to make pronunciation easier.

<table>
<tr><td colspan="5" align="center">leer to read</td></tr>
<tr><td>I read</td><td>leí</td><td>leímos</td><td>we read</td></tr>
<tr><td>you read (fam.)</td><td>leíste</td><td>leísteis</td><td>you read (pl. fam.)</td></tr>
<tr><td>you read (formal) }</td><td></td><td>leyeron</td><td>{ you read (pl. formal)
they read</td></tr>
<tr><td>he read
she read
it read }</td><td>leyó</td><td></td><td></td></tr>
</table>

 ## 20.1 HIGH-TECH COMMUNICATION

el fax/el facsímil	*the fax*	algo	*something*
el paquete	*package*	esta tarde	*this afternoon*
de	*from*	esta mañana	*this morning*
la computadora	*computer*	esta noche	*this evening*
el correo	*electronic mail,*	alguna vez	*once, ever*
electrónico	*E-mail*	la llamada de	*long-distance phone call*
la llamada	*phone call*	larga distancia	

 ## 20.2 LISTENING EXERCISE

Repeat each sentence after your instructor says it, reading along in the book as
you speak.

1. Vi a mis abuelos ayer.
2. Vi un programa muy interesante en la televisión esta mañana.
3. Vi a Juan en el club.
4. Vi a su mamá en el banco esta mañana.
5. Vi a su papá en el aeropuerto anoche.
6. Recibí un fax de la universidad.
7. Recibí una llamada muy importante anoche.
8. El doctor vendió el auto ayer.
9. Vendí la bicicleta.
10. Escribí las frases para la clase.
11. Escribí una carta esta mañana.
12. Recibí correo electrónico muy interesante esta mañana.
13. Recibí un regalo muy bonito ayer.
14. Mi papá recibió una llamada de larga distancia muy importante esta tarde.
15. María comprendió la lección.
16. Mamá recibió un regalo muy bonito ayer.

20.3 ORAL EXERCISE

Answer the following questions.

1. ¿Recibió usted un fax recientemente?
2. ¿Recibió usted un paquete esta semana?
3. ¿Recibió usted un regalo este mes?
4. ¿Qué fue el regalo?

5. ¿Recibió usted una llamada de larga distancia ayer?

6. ¿Recibió usted un correo electrónico esta semana?

7. ¿Escribió usted un correo electrónico esta semana?

8. ¿Qué hizo usted esta mañana?

9. ¿Escribió usted las frases para la clase?

10. ¿Escribió usted una carta ayer?

11. ¿Qué hizo usted esta tarde?

12. ¿Vendió usted un auto alguna vez?

13. ¿Salió usted con sus amigos esta semana?

14. ¿Dónde nació usted?

15. ¿En que año nació usted?

16. ¿Fue usted al cine anoche?

17. ¿Vio usted una película chistosa?

18. ¿Vio usted a su familia esta semana?

Can you do this exercise with your book closed?

20.4 ORAL OR WRITTEN EXERCISE

Give the you forms (singular) of the following verbs.

EXAMPLE: **comprender**
ANSWER: **comprendiste, comprendió**

1. vender	5. recibir
2. ver	6. insistir
3. nacer	7. decidir
4. vivir	8. escribir

20.5 ORAL EXERCISE

With another student, take turns asking and answering the questions provided.

1. ¿Recibió usted un fax este año?

2. ¿Recibió usted un correo electrónico esta semana?

3. ¿Recibió usted un paquete este mes?

4. ¿Recibió un regalo este mes?

5. ¿Vendió algo recientemente?

6. ¿Qué vendió?

7. ¿Escribió usted una composición ayer?

8. ¿Escribió un correo electrónico hoy?

9. ¿Escribió usted una carta este año?

10. ¿Vio a su mejor amigo(a) esta tarde?

11. ¿Vio a su compañero(a) de cuarto anoche?

12. ¿Qué comió para la cena anoche?

Grammar: Forming the past tense of all regular -er and -ir verbs

To form the past tense of all regular -er and -ir verbs, remove the **-er** or the **-ir** from the infinitive and add these endings.

Past tense endings of -er and -ir verbs

-í	-imos
-iste	-isteis
-ió	-ieron

comprender *to understand*

I understood	comprendí	comprendimos	we understood
you understood (fam.)	comprendiste	comprendisteis	you understood (pl.fam.)
you understood (formal) he understood she understood	comprendió	comprendieron	you understood (pl. formal) they understood

vivir *to live*

I lived	viví	vivimos	we lived
you lived (fam.)	viviste	vivisteis	you lived (pl. fam.)
you lived (formal) he lived she lived	vivió	vivieron	you lived (pl. formal) they lived

EX

Mis amigos y yo comprendimos la lección. — *My friends and I understood the lesson.*

Vivieron en San Diego por un año. — *You (pl. formal.) They lived in San Diego for a year.*

20.6 REVIEW–MINI-TEST

Give the past tense forms indicated of the following new **-er** and **-ir** verbs. You have never seen these verbs before but you can form the past tense easily because they are all regular.

EXAMPLE: **Yo/batir**   *to stir*
ANSWER: **Yo batí.**

1. **tú/prometer**   *to promise*
2. **ella/entender**   *to understand*
3. **yo/aprender**   *to learn*
4. **nosotros/
    discutir**   *to discuss,
                         to argue*

5. **tú y yo/abrir**   *to open*
6. **tú/sufrir**   *to suffer*
7. **ellos/subir**   *to go up, to climb*
8. **Uds./existir**   *to exist*

20.7 WHOM DID YOU SEE AT THE BANK?

me	*me*	**alto(a)**	*high, tall*
te	*you (fam.)*	**nuevo(a)**	*new*
lo	*him, you*	**a mí**	*to me*
la	*her, you*	**a ti**	*to you*
nos	*us*	**el otro día**	*the other day*
los, las	*you (pl.), them*	**la otra noche**	*the other night*
Lo vi.	*I saw him.*	**en el banco**	*in the bank*
La vi.	*I saw her.*	**mi tía**	*my aunt*
Lo vimos.	*We saw him.*	**¿Leyeron?**	*Did you (pl.) read?*
La vimos.	*We saw her.*	**Leímos.**	*We read.*
¿Nos vieron?	*Did you (pl.) see us?*	**¿Escribieron?**	*Did you (pl.) write?*
¿Me vieron?	*Did you (pl.) see me?*	**Escribimos.**	*We wrote.*
Te vi.	*I saw you.*	**¿Comprendieron?**	*Did you (pl.) understand?*
Los vi.	*I saw you (pl.)/them.*	**Comprendimos.**	*We understood.*
el menú/la lista	*menu, list*		

Grammar: Using direct object pronouns

A direct object is a noun that receives the action of a verb. To decide if a verb has a direct object, ask **whom?** or **what thing?** after the verb. The answer to that question is the direct object.

EXAMPLES:

Yo vi a María.	*(I saw whom?* **María**.*)* María is the direct object.
Yo leí un libro interesante.	*(I read what thing?* **un libro**.*)* **Un libro** is the direct object.

But:

Yo estoy contento.	*(I am what thing?)* There is no direct object in this sentence.

Sometimes, to avoid repeating words, the direct object is replaced with a direct object pronoun. The pronoun must match the direct object in number and gender.

EXAMPLES:

Vi a María anoche.	*La vi en el cine.*
Vi a mis abuelos ayer.	*Los vi en el teatro.*
Vi un programa hoy.	*Lo vi en la televisión.*

These are the direct object pronouns.

me	*me*	**nos**	*us*
te	*you (fam.)*	**los**	*you (pl.)(masc./masc. and fem).*
			them (masc./masc. and fem.)
lo	*you (masc.), him*	**las**	*you(pl.)(fem.only)*
la	*you (fem.), her*		*them (fem. only)*

EXAMPLES:

Me llamaron anoche.	*They called me last night.*
Te vi en el cine.	*I saw you at the theater.*
Lo vieron en la fiesta.	*They saw you (him) at the party.*
Nos llamó en enero.	*He (She, You) called us in January.*
Los vieron mucho.	*They saw them (you) often.*

20.8 ORAL EXERCISE

Answer the questions with the responses provided.

1. ¿Vio a Bernardo? Sí, lo vi ayer.
2. ¿Vio a María? Sí, la vi ayer.
3. ¿Vieron a Roberto y a Luis? Sí, los vimos.
4. ¿Vieron a Susana y a Elena? Sí, las vimos.
5. ¿Vieron al doctor y a la doctora? Sí, los vimos.
6. ¿Vieron a la doctora? Sí, la vimos.
7. ¿Vieron a mi papá? Sí, lo vimos.
8. ¿Vieron a mi mamá? Sí, la vimos.
9. ¿Vieron a mis abuelos? Sí, los vimos.
10. ¿Vieron a las niñas? Sí, las vimos.

Can you do this exercise with your book closed?

20.9 ORAL EXERCISE

With another student, take turns asking and answering the questions provided. Be sure to answer with a direct object pronoun.

EXAMPLE: **¿Compraste el auto ayer?**
ANSWER: **Sí, lo compré. No, no lo compré.**

1. ¿Viste a mi mamá esta mañana?
2. ¿Viste a mi papá anoche?
3. ¿Escribiste las frases para la clase?
4. ¿Leíste los libros para la clase?
5. ¿Leyeron el libro en la clase?
6. ¿Comprendiste la lección?
7. ¿Viste a mi amigo en el restaurante?
8. ¿Viste a Roberto en el teatro?
9. ¿Llamaste a tu tío anoche?
10. ¿Llamaste a tu mamá la semana pasada?

20.10 CONVERSATION VOCABULARY

Está enfermo.	*He's sick.*	Me va a dar...	*He's/She's going*
pobre	*poor (masc., fem.)*		*to give me...*
¡Qué terrible!	*How terrible!*	algunas píldoras	*some pills*
¿Qué tiene?	*What does he/she have?*	Voy a pasar a verlo(la).	*I'm going to drop by to see you (I'm going to pass by to see you).*
Tiene pulmonía.	*He/She has pneumonia.*	el antibiótico	*antibiotic*
¿Quién lo vio?	*Who saw him?*	Está mejor.	*He's/She's better.*
Estoy mejor.	*I'm better.*	su pulso	*your pulse*
Tengo fiebre.	*I have a fever.*	Vamos a ver.	*Let's see. We'll see.*
Estoy peor.	*I'm worse.*	Lo (la) van a curar.	*They are going to cure you.*
el termómetro	*thermometer*		
debajo de la lengua	*under the tongue*	Tome estas píldoras.	*Take these pills.*
por el dolor	*on account of the pain*	¿Cómo durmió?	*How did you sleep?*
		Dormí bien.	*I slept well.*
el (la) enfermero(a)	*the nurse*	No dormí muy bien.	*I didn't sleep very well.*
Me duele.	*It hurts (me).*	Cuídese.	*Take care of yourself.*
Me duelen.	*They hurt (me).*	para dormir	*in order to sleep*
Me duele la cabeza.	*My head aches (my head hurts me).*	Fue en ambulancia.	*He/She went in an ambulance.*
Me duelen los pulmones.	*My lungs hurt (my lungs hurt me).*	la garganta	*throat*
		el estómago	*stomach*
¿Te duele?	*Does it hurt you? (fam.)*	la mano	*hand*
		la pierna	*leg*
¿Le duele?	*Does it hurt you?*	el pie	*foot*
Le voy a dar...	*I'm going to give you...*	el brazo	*arm*
		la espalda	*back*

20.11 ORAL EXERCISE

Before you do the following exercise, take a few minutes to practice your adjectives.

	SINGULAR	PLURAL
good	bueno	buenos
	buena	buenas
bad	malo	malos
	mala	malas

beautiful,	lindo	lindos
lovely	linda	lindas
tired	cansado	cansados
	cansada	cansadas
sick	enfermo	enfermos
	enferma	enfermas

Now give the three other forms of each of the following adjectives.

1.	bonito	6.	linda
2.	alta	7.	enfermos
3.	buenos	8.	deliciosas
4.	malas	9.	nuevo
5.	cansado	10.	fantástica

20.12 CONVERSATION

The following block will serve as a guide for your conversation. Play the roles of Juan and María. However, do not restrict yourself only to what is in the block.

In the hospital

MARÍA: ¿Está enfermo Luis?

JUAN: Sí, pobre Luis, está muy enfermo. Está en el hospital. Entró en el hospital, en emergencia, a las tres de la mañana. Fue en ambulancia.

MARÍA: ¡Caramba! ¡Qué terrible! ¿Qué tiene?

JUAN: Tiene pulmonía. Tiene fiebre y le duele la cabeza.

MARÍA: ¿Quién lo vio?

JUAN: Lo vio el doctor Martínez.

MARÍA: ¿Es bueno el doctor Martínez?

JUAN: Sí, es muy bueno. Tiene una reputación excelente.

MARÍA: Pobre Luis. ¿Cómo está hoy?

JUAN: Está mejor. El doctor Martínez le dio antibióticos y unas píldoras para el dolor y para dormir.

Now, play the roles of Luis and the nurse (**enfermera**).

The following block will serve as a guide for your conversation. However, do not restrict yourself only to what is in the block.

The nurse and the patient

ENFERMERA: Buenos días, Luis. ¿Cómo está esta mañana?

LUIS: Buenos días, señorita. Esta mañana estoy mejor, pero me duelen mucho los pulmones y tengo fiebre.

ENFERMERA: Vamos a ver qué temperatura tiene. Aquí está el termómetro. Debajo de la lengua, por favor. Ahora voy a tomar su pulso.

LUIS: ¿Tengo fiebre?

ENFERMERA: Sí. Los antibióticos lo van a curar, pero es necesario esperar unos días.

LUIS: Me duele la cabeza.

ENFERMERA: Sí, es natural. Le voy a dar unas píldoras. ¿Cómo durmió anoche?

LUIS: No dormí muy bien, por el dolor.

ENFERMERA: Bueno, tome estas píldoras. Voy o pasar a verlo más tarde.

LUIS: Gracias, señorita. Adiós.

20.13 READING EXERCISE: VITAMINAS A TODAS HORAS

In this lesson, you learned to talk about health and sickness. Now read the advertisement on the following page for a product whose goal is to help people stay healthy. Use the words provided to help you understand the article, then answer the questions that follow.

durante	*during*	**el zumo**	*juice*
la merienda	*snack*	**gratis**	*free*
recién hechas	*recently made*		

1. What do you think the word **licuadora** means?
2. When does the ad suggest you drink juice?
3. What do you receive free if you buy this product?
4. Which item shown is the highest powered?
5. How does the headline (**Vitaminas a todas horas**) relate to the content of the ad?
6. What do you think the company's slogan (**Vitaminas recién hechas**) means?

Vitaminas a todas horas

con licuadoras Moulinex

En el desayuno. Después de la comida. Durante la merienda. O en la cena. Todas las horas son buenas para tomarse un vaso de vitaminas recién hechas. Porque lo sano y natural es beber fruta fresca. Y si quiere disfrutar de los mejores zumos, aproveche las frutas del tiempo; frutas que se encuentran en su época ideal de consumo. Y al mejor precio.

A todas horas también recordará a Moulinex. Porque ahora, por la compra de cualquiera de sus cuatro modelos de licuadoras, obtendrá **gratis un atractivo reloj de cocina**. Envíe el código de barras de la licuadora y sus datos personales al Aptdo de Correos 30288 - 08080 Barcelona. Recibirá el reloj en su domicilio. Y, además, pasará a ser **socio del Club Moulinex**, disfrutando de todas sus ventajas.

Licuadora 3   **Junior**
La familiar de más potencia   Con jarra incorporada

LICUADORAS
Moulinex®
Vitaminas recién hechas

20.14 WRITING EXERCISE

Imagine a scene in a doctor's office. There are three patients waiting to see the doctor. The nurse gathers information from each one about their illness. Write a conversation of 10–12 complete Spanish sentences.

VOCABULARY

NOUN

la ambulancia	ambulance	la lista	list, menu
el antibiótico	antibiotic	la llamada	phone call
el banco	bank	la llamada de	long-distance
el brazo	arm	larga distancia	phone call
la cabeza	head	la mano	hand
la computadora	computer	el menú	menu
el correo	electronic mail	el paquete	package
electrónico	(E-mail)	el pie	foot
el (la) enfer-	nurse	la pierna	leg
mero(a)		la píldora	pill
la espalda	back	los pulmones	lungs
el estómago	stomach	la pulmonía	pneumonia
el fax/el facsímil	fax	el pulso	pulse
la garganta	throat	el termómetro	thermometer
la lengua	tongue		

VERBS

insistir	to insist	ver	to see

ADJECTIVES

cansado(a)	tired
enfermo(a)	sick
lindo(a)	lovely, beautiful
mejor	better (masc., fem.)
peor	worse (masc., fem.)

OTHER WORDS AND EXPRESSIONS

a mí	*to me*	**Le voy a dar...**	*I'm going to give you...*
a ti	*to you*	**Lo (La) van**	*They are going to*
algo	*something*	**a curar.**	*cure you.*
alguna vez	*once, ever*	**¿Le duele?**	*Does it hurt you?*
algunos	*some*		*(singular form.)*
¿Cómo durmió?	*How did you sleep?*	**Me duele.**	*It hurts me.*
Cuídese.	*Take care of yourself.*	**Me duelen.**	*They hurt me.*
de	*from*	**Me va a dar...**	*He's/She's going to give me...*
debajo de	*beneath*	**No dormí**	*I didn't sleep very well.*
Dormí bien.	*I slept well.*	**muy bien.**	
la otra noche	*the other night*	**el otro día**	*the other day*
para dormir	*in order to sleep*	**¿Te duele?**	*Does it hurt you? (fam.)*
por el dolor	*on account of the*	**Tome estas**	*Take these pills.*
	pain	**píldoras.**	
¡Qué terrible!	*How terrible!*	**Vamos a ver.**	*Let's see. We'll see.*
		Voy a pasar	*I'm going to drop*
		a verlo(a).	*by to see you.*

OPTIONAL LIST

VERBS

abrir	*to open*	**existir**	*to exist*
aprender	*to learn*	**prometer**	*to promise*
batir	*to stir*	**subir**	*to go up, to climb*
discutir	*to discuss*	**sufrir**	*to suffer*
entender	*to understand*		

OTHER WORDS AND EXPRESSIONS

la	*you (fem.), her*	**los**	*you (pl.), them*
las	*you (pl.), them,*		*(masc./masc. and fem.)*
	(fem. only)	**me**	*me*
lo	*you (masc.), him*	**nos**	*us*
		te	*you (fam.)*

SPANISH-ENGLISH VOCABULARY

A

a, *to*
  a la, *at the, to the*
  a la luz, *by the light*
  a la una, *at one o'clock*
  ¿a qué hora? *at what time?*
  a tiempo, *on time*
  a veces, *at times*
abandonar, *to abandon*
abrigo, *m. coat*
abril, *April*
abrir, *to open*
absolutamente, *absolutely*
abuela, *f. grandmother*
abuelo, *m. grandfather*
abundante, *abundant*
acá, *here*
  ven acá, *come here*
Acapulco, *Acapulco*
accidental, *accidental*
accidente, *m. accident*
acción, *f. action*
aceptar, *to accept*
activa, *f. active*
actividad, *f. activity*
activo, *m. active*
acto, *m. act*
actor, *m. actor*
adiós, *good bye*
admirar, *to admire*
¿adónde? *(to) where?*
adoptar, *to adopt*
adorar, *to adore*
aduana, *f. customs*
aeropuerto, *m. airport*
afectar, *to affect*
África, *Africa*
agencia, *f. agency*
agente, *m. f. agent*
agosto, *August*
agua, *f. water*

¡ah!, *ah!*
ahora, *now, at this moment*
aire, *m. air*
ajustar, *to adjust*
ajuste, *adjust (command)*
al, *to the*
alarmar, *to alarm*
algo, *something*
alguna vez, *once, ever*
allí, *there*
  allí está, *there it is*
almuerzo, *m. lunch*
alquilar, *to rent*
alta, *f. high*
altas, *f. (pl.) tall, high*
alto, *m. high*
amarillo, *m. yellow*
ambición, *f. ambition*
ambulancia, *f. ambulance*
americana, *f. American*
americano, *m. American*
amiga, *f. friend*
amigo, *m. friend*
anaranjada, *f. orange*
anaranjado, *m. orange*
anduvimos, *we walked, we rode*
animal, *m. animal*
aniversario, *m. anniversary*
anoche, *last night*
antena parabólica, *f. satellite dish*
antibiótico, *m. antibiotic*
año, *m. year*
aprender, *to learn*
árbol, *m. tree*
argentina, *f. Argentine*
argentino, *m. Argentine*
aristocracia, *f. aristocracy*
arquitecto, *m. architect*
arroz, *m. rice*
artículo, *m. article*
artista, *m. & f. artist*
asiento, *m. seat*

aspecto, *m. aspect*
aspirina, *f. aspirin*
astronauta, *m. f. astronaut*
atención, *f. attention*
aterrizar, *to land (in an airplane)*
Atlántico, *m. Atlantic*
atómica, *f. atomic*
atómico, *m. atomic*
atractiva, *f. attractive*
atractivo, *m. attractive*
atrocidad, *f. atrocity*
atún, *m. tuna fish*
auto, *m. car, auto*
autobús, *m. bus*
aviación, *f. aviation*
avión, *m. airplane*
¡ay!, *oh, ouch*
ayer, *yesterday*
ayudar, *to help, to aid*
ayudó, *he, she, it helped*
  me ayudó, *he, she, it helped me*
azúcar, *m. sugar*
azul, *m. & f. blue*

B

bailar, *to dance*
baloncesto, *m. basketball*
banco, *m. bank*
baño, *m. bath, bathroom*
  baño de sol, *sun bath*
batir, *to stir*
béisbol, *m. baseball*
bicicleta, *f. bicycle*
bien, *well, fine*
bistec, *m. beefsteak*
billete, *m. ticket*
blanca, *f. white*
blanco, *m. white*
blusa, *f. blouse*
Bogotá, *Bogota*

boleto, *m. ticket*
boliviana, *f. Bolivian*
boliviano, *m. Bolivian*
bonita, *f. pretty*
bonito, *m. pretty*
bosque, *m. forest*
brazo, *m. arm*
bridge, *m. bridge (game)*
buena, *f. (sing.) good*
buenas, *f. (pl.) good*
　　buenas noches, *good
　　evening, good night*
　　buenas tardes, *good afternoon*
bueno, *m. (sing.) good, hello (phone)*
buenos, *m. (pl.) good*
　　buenos días, *good morning*

C

cabaña, *f. cabin*
cabeza, *f. head*
café, *m. coffee*
calcetines, *m. socks*
calor, *m. heat*
　　hace calor, *it's hot*
cama, *f. bed*
caminar, *to walk*
camión, *m. truck*
camisa, *f. shirt*
campo, *m. country (not nation)*
canal, *m. canal*
canario, *m. canary*
canción, *f. song*
candor, *m. candor*
cansada, *f. tired*
cansado, *m. tired*
cantar, *to sing*
capacidad, *f. capacity*
capitalista, *m. f. capitalist*
Caracas, *Caracas*
¡caramba! *gee whiz!, gosh!, darn*
caramelos, *m. (pl.) hard candy*
carne, *f. meat*
carta, *f. letter*
casa, *f. house*
　　en casa, *at home*
casete, *f. cassette, tape*
catorce, *fourteen*
causar, *to cause*

cebolla, *f. onion*
celebración, *f. celebration*
celebrar, *to celebrate*
cena, *f. supper*
central, *m. & f. central*
centro, *m. middle, center, downtown*
cerca, *close, near*
　　cerca de, *close to*
cereal, *m. cereal*
cero, *m. zero*
chicle, *m. chewing gum*
chile, *m. chili, chili peppers*
chilena, *f. Chilean*
chileno, *m. Chilean*
chiquitito, *m. very, very little*
chistoso, *m. funny*
chocolate, *m. chocolate (drink)*
chocolates, *m. chocolates (candy)*
chuleta, *f. chop*
　　chuleta de puerco, *pork
　　chop*
cielo, *m. sky*
cien, *one hundred*
científico, *m. scientific*
cinco, *five*
cincuenta, *fifty*
cine, *m. movies, movie theater*
cinta, *f. cassette, tape*
cinturón, *m. belt, seat belt*
ciudad, *f. city*
clase, *f. class*
cliente, *m. & f. client*
club, *m. club*
coche, *m. car*
cocina, *f. kitchen, cuisine*
cocinar, *to cook*
cocinera, *f. cook, chef*
cocinero, *m. cook, chef*
cóctel, *m. cocktail*
colección, *f. collection*
colombiana, *f. Colombian*
colombiano, *m. Colombian*
colonial, *m. & f. colonial*
color, *m. color*
　　color café, *brown*
combinación, *f. combination*
combinar, *to combine*
comedia, *f. comedy*
comer, *to eat*

comercial, *commercial*
comida, *f. meal, dinner, food*
como, *as, I eat*
¿cómo? *how?*
　　¿cómo no? *how not?*
cómodo, *m. comfortable*
compañera de cuarto, *f. room-
　　mate*
compañero de cuarto, *m.
　　roommate*
comparar, *to compare*
competente, *m. & f. competent*
completamente, *completely*
completo, *m. complete*
complexión, *f. complexion*
composición, *f. composition*
comprar, *to buy*
compras, *f. (pl.) purchases,
　　shopping*
　　voy de compras, *I'm going
　　shopping*
comprender, *to understand*
comprendo, *I understand*
compro, *I buy*
computadora, *f. computer*
comunicación, *f. communication*
comunicar, *to communicate*
comunidad, *f. community*
con, *with*
con ellos, *with them*
concentración, *f. concentration*
concentrar, *to concentrate*
concierto, *m. concert*
condición, *f. condition*
conductor, *m. conductor
　　(train)*
conectar, *to connect*
conferencia, *f. conference, lecture*
confusión, *f. confusion*
conmigo, *with me*
consistir, *to consist*
constante, *m. & f. constant*
constitución, *f. constitution*
constructiva, *f. constructive*
constructivo, *m. constructive*
contacto, *m. contact*
contenta, *f. happy*
contento, *m. happy*
contestar, *to answer, to reply*

contigo, *with you*
continente, *m. continent*
contraria, *f. contrary*
contrario, *m. contrary*
contribución, *f. contribution*
conveniente, *m. & f. convenient*
conversación, *f. conversation*
conversar, *to converse*
copiar, *to copy*
corbata, *f. necktie*
correcta, *f. correct*
correcto, *m. correct*
correo electrónico, *m. electronic
mail, e-mail*
correr, *to run*
cosa, *f. thing*
creer, *to believe, to think*
crema, *f. cream*
criminal, *m. & f. criminal*
¿cuándo?, *when?*
cuarenta, *forty*
cuarenta y uno, *forty-one*
cuarto, *m. quarter, room*
cuatro, *four*
cuatrocientos, *four hundred*
cubana, *f. Cuban*
cubano, *m. Cuban*
cuidar, *to take care of*
cuídese, *take care of yourself*
cultivar, *to cultivate*
cultural, *cultural*
curar, *to cure*
curiosa, *f. curious*
curiosidad, *f. curiosity*
curioso, *m. curious*

D

dar, *to give*
   dar una clase, *to teach or to
take a class*
de, *of, from, about*
   de nada, *you're welcome*
debajo, *under*
decente, *m. & f. decent*
decidir, *to decide*
decir, *to say, to tell*
decisión, *f. decision*
declarar, *to declare*

defecto, *m. defect*
del, *m. of the*
deliciosa, *f. delicious*
delicioso, *m. delicious*
democracia, *f. democracy*
democrática, *f. democratic*
democrático, *m. democratic*
dentista, *m. dentist*
depositar, *to deposit*
desayuno, *m. breakfast*
describir, *to describe*
descripción, *f. description*
descriptiva, *f. descriptive*
descriptivo, *m. descriptive*
despacho, *m. office*
despegar, *to take off*
después, *after, afterward*
destructiva, *f. destructive*
destructivo, *m. destructive*
di, *I gave*
día, *m. day*
   todo el día, *all day long*
días, *m. days*
   todos los dias, *everyday*
diccionario, *m. dictionary*
diciembre, *December*
dictar, *to dictate*
diecinueve, *nineteen*
dieciocho, *eighteen*
dieciséis, *sixteen*
diecisiete, *seventeen*
diez, *ten*
diferencia, *f. difference*
diferente, *m. & f. different*
dignidad, *f. dignity*
dije, *I said*
dinamita, *f. dynamite*
dinero, *m. money*
diploma, *m. diploma*
diplomacia, *f. diplomacy*
diplomática, *f. diplomatic*
diplomático, *m. diplomatic*
directa, *f. direct*
directamente, *directly*
directo, *m. direct*
director, *m. director*
disciplina, *f. discipline*
disco compacto, *m. compact
disc, CD*

discutir, *to argue*
distancia, *f. distance*
dividir, *to divide*
división, *f. division*
doce, *twelve*
doctor, *m. doctor*
doctora, *f. doctor*
dolor, *m. pain*
domingo, *m. Sunday*
dominicana, *f. Dominican*
dominicano, *m. Dominican*
¿dónde?, *where?*
dormí, *I slept*
dormir, *to sleep*
dos, *two*
doscientos, *two hundred*
drama, *m, drama*
dramática, *f. dramatic*
dramático, *m. dramatic*
duele, *hurts, aches*
   me duele, *it hurts me*
   me duelen, *they hurt
me*
dulces (los), *m. (pl.)
candy*
durmió, *slept*

E

economista, *m. & f. economist*
edificio, *m. building*
editorial, *m. & f. editorial*
efectiva, *f. effective*
efectivo, *m. effective*
efecto, *m. effect*
el, *m. the*
elástico, *m. elastic*
elección, *f. election*
eléctrica, *f. electric*
electricidad, *f. electricity*
eléctrico, *m. electric*
elefante, *m. elephant*
elegancia, *f. elegance*
elegante, *m. & f. elegant*
elemental, *elemental*
ellos *m. they, them*
   con ellos, *with them*
emblema, *m. emblem*
emergencia, *f. emergency*

emoción, *f. emotion*

en, *m., on*

en casa, *at home*

enfrente de, *in front of*

enchilada, *f. enchilada*

encontrar, *to find, meet*

enero, *January*

enferma, *f. sick*

enfermera, *f. nurse*

enfermero, *m. nurse*

enfermo, *m. sick*

ensalada, *f. salad*

entender, *to understand*

entrar, *to enter, to go in, to come in*

entusiasmo, *m. enthusiasm*

equipaje, *m. luggage*

error, *m. error*

es, *is*

es de, *he/she is from*

esa, *f. that*

escapar, *to escape*

escriba, *write (command)*

escribir, *to write*

escribo, *I write*

escuela, *f. school*

eso, *m. that*

espacio, *m. space*

espalda, *f. back*

español, *m. Spanish (language),*
m. Spaniard

española, *f. Spaniard*

espárragos, *m. asparagus*

espera, *f. waiting (adj.)*

esperar, *to hope, wait, expect*

esta, *f. this*

está, *you are, he, she, it is, are*
you? is he, she, it?

estación, *f. station*

estacionar, *to park*

estamos, *we are*

están, *you (pl.) are, they are*

estar, *to be*

estatua, *f. statue*

estéreo, *m. stereo*

estómago, *m. stomach*

estoy, *I am*

estrella, *f. star*

estudiando, *studying*

estudiante, *m. & f. student*

estudiar, *to study*

estudio, *I study*

estuve, *I was*

eternidad, *f. eternity*

evadir, *to evade*

evidencia, *f. evidence*

evidente, *m. & f. evident*

exacta, *f. exact*

exacto, *m. exact*

examinar, *to examine*

excelencia, *f. excellence*

excelente, *m. & f. excellent*

exclusiva, *f. exclusive*

exclusivo, *m. exclusive*

existir, *to exist*

expansión, *f. expansion*

experiencia, *f. experience*

experimentación, *f.*
experimentation

experimental, *m. & f. experimental*

experimentar, *to experiment*

exploración, *f. exploration*

explorar, *to explore*

explosión, *f. explosion*

explosiva, *f. explosive*

explosivo, *m. explosive*

exportar, *to export*

expresar, *to express*

expresión, *f. expression*

expresiva, *f. expressive*

expresivo, *m. expressive*

exterior, *m. & f. exterior*

extracto, *m. extract*

extraordinaria, *f. extraordinary*

extraordinario, *m. extraordinary*

F

fabulosa, *f. fabulous*

fabuloso, *m. fabulous*

facsímil, *m. fax*

factoría, *f. factory*

falda *f. skirt*

familia, *f. family*

famosa, *f. famous*

famoso, *m. famous*

fantástica, *f. fantastic, "terrific"*

fantástico, *m. fantastic, "terrific"*

farmacia, *f. drugstore, pharmacy*

favor, *m. favor*

fax, *m. fax*

febrero, *February*

federal, *m. & f. federal*

festival, *m. festival*

fiebre, *f. fever*

fiesta, *f. party*

fin, *m. end*

el fin de semana, *weekend*

final, *m. & f. final*

finalmente, *finally*

flexible, *m. & f. flexible*

flor, *f. flower*

flotar, *to float*

formal, *m. & f. formal*

formar, *to form*

formalidad, *f. formality*

fortuna, *f. fortune*

por fortuna, *fortunately*

fotografía, *f. photograph*

Francia, *France*

frase, *f. sentence, phrase*

frecuencia, *f. frequence*

frente, *f. forehead; adv. front*

fresas, *f. (pl.) strawberries*

fresca, *f. fresh, cool*

frío, *m. cold*

frito, *m. fried*

frivolidad, *f. frivolity*

frustrar, *to frustrate*

fruta, *f. fruit*

fue, *you, he, she, it went*

fueron, *you (pl.) went, they went*

fui, *I went*

fui de compras, *I went*
shopping

fuimos, *we went*

fuman, *you (pl.) smoke, they smoke*

fumar, *to smoke*

furiosa, *f. furious*

furioso, *m. furious*

fútbol, *m. soccer*

G

galopar, *to gallop*

ganar, *to win, to earn*

garaje, *m. garage*

garganta, *f. throat*

gasolina, *f. gasoline*
gatita, *f. kitten, little cat*
gatito, *m. kitten, little cat*
gato, *m. cat*
gelatina, *f. gelatine*
general, *adj. general, usual*
general, *m. general*
generalmente, *generally*
generosa, *f. generous*
generoso, *m. generous*
gente, *f. people*
geranio, *m. geranium*
gimnasia, *f. gymnastics*
golf, *m. golf*
gracia, *f. grace*
gracias, *thank you*
gradual, *m. & f. gradual*
grande, *m. & f. big*
gris, *m. & f. grey*
guantes, *m. (pl.) gloves*
guitarra, *f. guitar*
guitarrista, *m. guitar player*
gusta, *(sing.) like*
    me gusta, *I like it, I like . . .*
    le gusta, *you like, he, she, it
    likes . . .*
    nos gusta, *we like*
gustan, *(pl.) like*
    me gustan, *I like (something
    plural)*
gustar, *to like*

H

hablar, *to speak*
hablo, *I speak*
hace *he, she, it does, makes, you
    do, make*
    hace calor, *it's hot*
    hace frío, *it's cold*
    hace una hora, *an hour ago*
hacer, *to do, to make*
haces, *you make, do you make?
    you do, do you do? (fam.)*
hago, *I do, I make*
hay, *there is, there are, is there?, are
    there?*
helada, *f. ice cream*
helado, *m. ice cream*

hermana, *f. sister*
hermano, *m. brother*
hice, *I did, I made*
hizo, *you, he, she, it did, made*
hombre, *m. man*
honor, *m. honor*
hora, *f. hour*
    ¿a qué hora? *at what time?*
horizontal, *horizontal*
horrible, *m. & f. horrible*
horror, *m. horror*
hospital, *m. hospital*
hospitalidad, *f. hospitality*
hotel, *m. hotel*
hoy, *today*
huevo, *m. egg*
humanidad, *f. humanity*
humor, *m. humor*

I

idea *f. idea*
ideal, *m. & f. ideal*
idealista, *m. & f. idealist*
iglesia, *f. church*
ignorante, *m. & f. ignorant*
importancia, *f. importance*
importante, *m. & f. important*
importar, *to import*
imposible, *m. & f. impossible*
impresión, *f. impression*
incidente, *m. incident*
independencia, *f. independence*
indiferencia, *f. indifference*
indirecta, *f. indirect*
indirecto, *m. indirect*
industrial, *m. & f. industrial*
inevitable, *m. & f. inevitable*
inferior, *m. & f, inferior*
inglés, *m. English*
inmensa, *f. immense*
inmenso, *m. immense*
inocencia, *f. innocence*
insecto, *m. insect*
insistir, *to insist*
inspirar, *to inspire*
instante, *m. instant*
instructor, *m. instructor*
instrumental, *instrumental*

instrumento, *m. instrument*
intelecto, *m. intellect*
inteligencia, *f. intelligence*
inteligente, *m. & f. intelligent*
intención, *f. intention*
interesante, *m. & f. interesting*
interior, *interior*
inventar, *to invent*
inventor, *m. inventor*
invierno, *m. winter*
invisible, *m. & f. invisible*
invitación, *f. invitation*
invitar, *to invite*
ir, *to go*
irresistible, *m. & f. irresistible*
isla, *f. island*
italiana, *f. Italian*
italiano, *m. Italian*
italianos, *m. Italians*

J

jamón, *m. ham*
jardín, *m. garden*
jueves, *m. Thursday*
jugando, *playing (a game)*
jugar, *to play*
jugo, *m. juice*
    jugo de naranja, *m. orange
    juice*
julio, *July*
junio, *June*
justicia, *f. justice*

L

la, *f. the*
la, *f. her, you, it*
laboratorio, *m. laboratory*
lago, *m. lake*
lancha, *f. boat, launch*
    lancha de motor, *motor boat*
lápiz, *m. pencil*
las, *f. (pl.) the*
las, *f. them*
lavar, *to wash*
le, *pr. you, him, her, it*
    ¿le gusta? *do you like?*
lección, *f. lesson*

leche, *f. milk*
lechuga, *f. lettuce*
leer, *to read*
legal, *m. & f. legal*
lengua *f. language, tongue*
leo, *I read*
león, *m. lion*
les, *to them, to you (pl.)*
levantar, *to raise, to lift*
librería, *f. bookstore*
libro, *m. book*
limón, *m. lemon*
limonada, *f. lemonade*
limpiar, *to clean*
linda, *f. lovely, beautiful*
lindo, *m. lovely, beautiful*
lista, *f. list, menu*
lista, *f. ready*
listo, *m. ready*
literaria, *f. literary*
literario, *m. literary*
literatura, *f. literature*
llamada, *f. phone call*
   llamada de larga distancia,
    f. long distance phone call
llamar, *to call*
llave, *f. key*
llega, *he, she, it arrives*
llegar, *to arrive, get here, get there*
llevar, *to take, to carry*
llevarla, *to take her, it*
llevarlo, *to take him, it*
llevaste, *you took (fam.)*
lo, *m. him, you, it*
loca, *f. crazy*
local, *m. & f. local*
loco, *m. crazy, mad*
locura, *f. madness*
los, *m. (pl.) the*
los, *m. them*
lubricante, *m. lubricant*
luna, *f. moon*
lunes, *m. Monday*
luz, *f. light*

M

macarrones, *m. (pl.) macaroni*
maletera, *f. red-cap, porter*

maletero, *m. red-cap, porter*
mamá, *f. mother*
mandar, *to send*
mano, *f. hand*
mansión, *f. mansion*
manual, *manual*
manzana, *f. apple*
mañana, *f. morning, tomorrow*
mar, *m. sea*
marchar, *to march*
mariposa, *f. butterfly*
marrón, *brown*
martes, *m. Tuesday*
marzo, *March*
más, *more*
   más tarde, *later*
mayo, *May*
mayonesa, *mayonnaise*
me, *me, to me*
media, *f. half*
   media hora, *half an hour*
medicina, *f. medicine*
mejor, *m. & f. better*
melón, *m. melon, cantaloupe*
menú, *m. menu*
mercado, *m. market*
mes, *m. month*
mesa, *f. table*
metal, *m. metal*
mexicana, *f. Mexican*
mexicano, *m. Mexican*
mi, *my*
mí, *me*
miércoles, *m. Wednesday*
mil, *one thousand*
millones, *millions*
minuto, *m. minute*
¡mira! *look!*
misma, *f. same*
mismo, *m. same*
misteriosa, *f. mysterious*
misterioso, *m. mysterious*
moderna, *f. modern*
moderno, *m. modern*
momento, *m. moment*
montaña, *f. mountain*
morada, *f. purple*
morado, *m. purple*
moral, *moral*

moralidad, *f. morality*
mosquito, *m. mosquito*
motocicleta, *f. motorcycle*
motor, *m. motor*
mucha, *f. much, a lot*
muchas, *f. (pl.) many, a lot*
muchísimo, *m. very, very much*
mucho, *m. much, a lot*
muchos, *m. (pl.) many, a lot*
mujer, *f. woman*
mundo, *m. world*
municipalidad, *f. municipality*
museo, *m. museum*
música, *f. music*
musical, *musical*
músico, *f. music*
muy, *very*

N

nacer, *to be born*
nación, *f. nation*
nacionalidad, *f. nationality*
nada, *nothing*
nadar, *to swim*
nado, *I swim*
naipes (los), *m. (pl.) cards*
naranja, *f. orange*
nativa, *f. native*
nativo, *m. native*
natural, *m. & f. natural*
naturalmente, *naturally*
naval, *naval*
necesaria, *f. necessary*
necesario, *m. necessary*
necesidad, *f. necessity, need*
necesitar, *to need*
necesito, *I need*
negativa, *f. negative*
negativo, *m. negative*
negra, *f. black*
negro, *m. black*
niña, *f. girl*
niño, *m. boy*
niños, *m. (pl.) children*
no, *no, not*
noble, *m. & f. noble*
noche, *f. night*
noches, *f. (pl.) nights*

nombre, *m. name*
nos, *us*
nosotras, *f. we*
nosotros, *m. we*
notar, *to notice*
novecientos, *nine hundred*
novela, *f. novel*
novelista, *m. & f. novelist*
noventa, *ninety*
noviembre, *November*
nuestros, *m. (pl.) our*
nueve, *nine*
nuevo, *m. new*
número, *m. number*

O

o, *or*
obscuridad, *f. darkness, obscurity*
océano, *m. ocean*
Océano Pacífico, *m. Pacific Ocean*
ochenta, *eighty*
ocho, *eight*
ochocientos, *eight hundred*
octubre, *October*
ocupada, *f. busy*
ocupado, *m. busy*
ofender, *to offend*
ofensiva, *f. offensive*
ofensivo, *m. offensive*
oficina, *f. office*
once, *eleven*
optimista, *m. & f. optimist*
ordinaria, *f. ordinary*
ordinario, *m. ordinary*
organista, *m. & f. organist*
original, *m. & f. original*
otoño, *m. autumn*
otra, *f. other, another*
otro, *m. other, another*
oye, *listen*

P

paciente, *m. f. patient*
Pacífico, *m. Pacific*
país, *m. country (nation)*

pájaro, *m. bird*
paloma, *f. dove, pigeon*
pan, *m. bread*
    pan tostado, *m. toast*
panameña, *f. Panamanian*
panameño, *m. Panamanian*
panorama, *m. panorama*
pantalones, *m. (pl.) trousers, pants*
papá, *m. father*
papas, *f. potatoes*
paquete, *m. package*
para, *for, in order to*
paraguas, *m. umbrella*
parar, *to stop*
parque, *m. park*
pasado, *m. past*
pasaporte, *m. passport*
pasar, *to pass, to spend (time)*
pase, *come in*
    pase por aquí, *step this way*
patente, *m. patent*
penicilina, *f. penicillin*
pensión, *f. pension*
peor, *m. & f. worse*
pera, *f. pear*
perdón, *pardon me, excuse me*
perfecta, *f. perfect*
perfecto, *m. perfect*
periódico, *m. newspaper*
periodista, *m. journalist*
permanente, *m. & f. permanent*
permitir, *to allow, to permit*
pero, *but*
perro, *m. dog*
persistencia, *f. persistence*
persistir, *to persist*
persona, *f. person*
personal, *m. & f. personal*
personalidad, *f. personality*
persuadir, *to persuade*
pesimista, *m. & f. pessimist*
pianista, *m. & f. pianist*
piano, *m. piano*
pie, *m. foot*
pierna, *f. leg*
píldora, *f. pill*
pimienta, *f. pepper (black)*
pintar, *to paint*

pintura, *f. painting*
pipa, *f. pipe*
piscina, *f. swimming pool*
planeta, *m. planet*
planta, *f. plant*
plantar, *to plant*
plato, *m. plate, dish*
playa, *f. beach*
pluma, *f. pen*
plural, *m. & f. plural*
pobre, *m. & f. poor*
poca, *f. a little bit*
poco, *m. a little bit*
poema, *m. poem*
pollo, *m. chicken*
pone, *you put, he, she, it puts*
poner, *to put*
pongo, *I put*
popular, *m. & f. popular*
por, *by*
    por favor, *please*
    ¿por qué?, *why?*
    por teléfono, *on the phone*
porque, *because*
portero, *m. doorman*
posibilidad, *f. possibility*
posible, *m. & f. possible*
posiblemente, *possibly*
postal, *m. postcard*
postre, *m. dessert*
practicar, *to practice*
preciosa, *f. precious*
precioso, *m. precious*
preparación, *f. preparation*
preparar, *to prepare*
presentación, *f. presentation*
presentar, *to present*
presente, *m. & f. present*
presento, *I present, introduce*
    te presento, *allow me to introduce*
presidente, *m. & f. president*
primaria, *f. primary*
primario, *m. primary*
primavera, *f. spring*
primitiva, *f. primitive*
primitivo, *m. primitive*
primo, *m. cousin*
probable, *m. & f. probable*

probablemente, _probably_
problema, _m. problem_
productiva, _f. productive_
productivo, _m. productive_
producto, _m. product_
profesor, _m. professor_
profesora, _f. professor_
programa, _m. program_
progresar, _to progress_
progresiva, _f. progressive_
progresivo, _m. progressive_
progreso, _I progress_
prometer, _to promise_
prominente, _m. & f. prominent_
pronto, _quickly, soon_
prosperidad, _f. prosperity_
protector, _m. protector_
protestar, _to protest_
prudente, _m. & f. prudent_
publicidad, _f. publicity_
público, _m. public_
puerta, _f. door_
Puerto Rico, _Puerto Rico_
puertorriqueña, _f. Puerto Rican_
puertorriqueño, _m. Puerto Rican_
pulmonía, _f. pneumonia_
pulso, _m. pulse_

Q

¡qué! _how!_
¿qué? _what?_
que, _that, than_
¡qué bueno! _how good!, great!_
querer, _to want, to love_
quesadilla, _f. quesadilla_
queso, _m. cheese_
¿quién?, _who?_
¿quieres? _do you want?_
¿quieres ir? _do you want to go?_
quiero, _I want, I love_
quince, _fifteen_
quinientos, _five hundred_

R

radio, _m. radio_
rancho, _m. ranch_

realidad, _f. reality_
recibir, _to receive, to meet_
recibirla, _to meet her_
recibirlo, _to meet him_
recibo, _I receive_
recomendación, _f. recommendation_
recomendar, _to recommend_
reflector, _m. reflector_
reflexión, _f. reflection_
refrigerador, _m. refrigerator_
regalo, _m. present_
regresar, _to return, to get back, to come back_
religiosa, _f. religious_
religioso, _m. religious_
reloj, _m. clock, watch_
representación, _f. representation_
representar, _to represent_
reputación, _f. reputation_
reservar, _to reserve_
residencial, _residential_
resistir, _to resist_
responsable, _m. & f. responsible_
restaurante, _m. restaurant_
resto, _m. (the) rest_
revelación, _f. revelation_
revolución, _f. revolution_
rica, _f. tasty, rich_
rico, _m. tasty, rich_
ridícula, _f. ridiculous_
ridículo, _m. ridiculous_
río, _m. river_
rival, _m. rival_
roja, _f. red_
rojo, _m. red_
romántica, _f. romantic_
romántico, _m. romantic_
rosa, _f. rose_
rosada, _f. pink_
rosado, _m. pink_
rosario, _m. rosary_
rosbif, _m. roast beef_
rumor, _m. rumor_
rural, _rural_
rusa, _f. Russian_
ruso, _m. Russian_
rusos, _m. Russians_

S

sábado, _m. Saturday_
sal, _f. salt_
sala, _f. living room_
sala de espera, _waiting room_
sale, _goes out, leaves (a place)_
salgo, _I go out, I leave (a place)_
salir, _to go out, to leave (a place)_
salmón, _m. salmon_
saltar, _to jump_
salvación, _f. salvation_
salvar, _to save_
sándwich, _m. sandwich_
sardina, _f. sardine_
sé, _I know_
secretaria, _f. secretary_
secretario, _m. secretary_
seis, _six_
seiscientos, _six hundred_
semana, _f. week_
señor, _m. mister, sir_
señora, _f. Mrs., madam_
señorita, _f. young lady, Miss_
separación, _f. separation_
separar, _to separate_
septiembre, _September_
serenata, _f. serenade_
sesenta, _sixty_
setecientos, _seven hundred_
setenta, _seventy_
sí, _yes_
si, _if_
siempre, _always_
significante, _significant_
simpática, _f. nice_
simpático, _m. nice_
sinceridad, _f. sincerity_
siete, _seven_
social, _social_
socialista, _m. & f. socialist_
sociedad, _f. society_
sofá, _m. sofa_
sol, _m. sun_
sola, _f. alone_
solitaria, _f. solitary_
solitario, _m. solitary_
solo, _m. alone, music (solo)_
sombrero, _m. hat_

son, *(pl.) are*
sopa, *f. soup*
su, *your, his, her, their*
subir, *to go up, to climb*
suéter, *m. sweater*
suficiente, *m. & f. enough*
sufrir, *to suffer*
superior, *superior*
supermercado, *m. supermarket*
sus, *their (pl.)*

T

taco, *m. taco*
también, *too, also*
tarde, *late*
tarde, *f. afternoon*
taxi, *m. taxi*
taza, *f. cup*
te, *you, to you (fam.)*
té, *m. tea*
teatro, *m. theater*
teléfono, *m. telephone*
televisor, *m. television set*
televisión, *f. television*
temperatura, *f. temperature*
temporaria, *f. temporary*
temporario, *m. temporary*
temprano, *early*
tendencia, *f. tendency*
tenemos, *we have*
tener, *to have*
tengo, *I have*
tenis, *m. tennis*
tenor, *m. tenor*
terminar, *to finish*
termómetro, *m. thermometer*
terraza, *f. terrace*
terrible, *m. & f. terrible*
terror, *m. terror*
tía, *f. aunt*
tiempo, *m. time*
tienda, *f. store*
    tienda de ropa, *f. clothing store*
tiene, *you have, he, she, it has*
tienen, *you (pl.) have, they have*
tierra, *f. earth*
tigre, *m. tiger*

tío, *m. uncle*
típico, *m. typical*
tocar, *to touch, to play (an instrument)*
tocino, *m. bacon*
toda, *f. all, every*
    toda la mañana, *all morning*
todas, *f. every*
todo, *m. all*
    todo el día, *all day long*
todos, *m. every; everybody*
    todos los días, *everyday*
tolerancia, *f. tolerance*
tolerante, *tolerant*
tomar, *to take, to have (food)*
tomate, *m. tomato*
tome, *take (command)*
tomo, *I take*
tónico, *m. tonic*
torero, *m. bullfighter*
toro, *m. bull*
tostada, *f. toasted, toast*
tostador electrónico, *m. electric toaster*
total, *total*
trabajar, *to work*
trabajo, *m. work (noun)*
trabajo, *I work*
tractor, *m. tractor*
traer, *to bring*
tráfico, *m. traffic*
traigo, *I bring*
traje, *I brought*
traje, *m. suit (man's or woman's)*
trajo, *you, he, she, it brought*
transparente, *m. & f. transparent*
trece, *thirteen*
treinta y uno, *thirty-one*
treinta, *thirty*
tren, *m. train*
tres, *three*
trescientos, *three hundred*
trinidad, *f. trinity*
triste, *m. & f. sad*
tropical, *m. & f. tropical*
trotar, *to trot, to jog*
tu, *your (fam.)*

tú, *m. & f. you (fam.)*
tulipán, *m. tulip*
tumor, *m. tumor*
turista, *m. & f. tourist*
tuve, *I had*

U

un, *a, an (masc.)*
una, *a, an (fem.)*
una, *f. one*
universal, *universal*
universidad, *f. university*
uno, *one*
unos días, *a few days*
unos, *m. (pl.) some*
urgencia, *f. urgency*
urgente, *m. & f. urgent*
usar, *to use*
usted, *you (sing.)*
ustedes, *you (pl.)*
uvas, *f. (pl.) grapes*

V

va, *you go, he, she, it goes, you are going, he, she, it is going*
vacaciones, *f. (pl.) vacation*
valiente, *m. & f. brave*
valija, *f. suitcase*
valle, *m. valley*
vamos, *we go, we are going, let's go*
van, *you (pl.) go, they go, you (pl.) are going, they are going*
vapor, *m. vapor, steam*
variedad, *f. variety*
vas, *you go, are you going? (fam.)*
    vas a ver, *you'll see, are you going to see?*
vaselina, *f. vaseline*
vaya, *go (command)*
veces, *f. (pl.) times*
veinte, *twenty*
veinticinco, *twenty-five*
veinticuatro, *twenty-four*
veintidós, *twenty-two*
veintinueve, *twenty-nine*
veintiocho, *twenty-eight*
veintiséis, *twenty-six*

veintisiete, *twenty-seven*

veintitrés, *twenty-three*

veintiuno, *twenty-one*

velocidad, *f. velocity, speed*

ven, *come*

    ven acá, *come here*

vender, *to sell*

vendo, *I sell*

venezolana, *f. Venezuelan*

venezolano, *m. Venezuelan*

vengo, *I come*

venir, *to come*

ventilación, *f. ventilation*

veo, *I see*

ver, *to see*

verano, *m. summer*

¿verdad? *true? isn't that so?*

verdad, *f. truth, true*

verde, *m. & f. green*

verduras, *f. (pl.) vegetables*

verlo, *to see you, him, it*

verte, *to see you*

vertical, *vertical*

vestido, *m. dress*

veterinaria, *f. veterinary*

veterinario, *m. veterinary*

vi, *I saw*

viajar, *to travel*

victoriosa, *f. victorious*

victorioso, *m. victorious*

videojuego, *m. videogame*

viejo, *m. old*

viene, *you come, he, she, it comes*

viernes, *m. Friday*

vigor, *m. vigor*

vine, *I came*

violencia, *f. violence*

violeta, *f. violet*

violín, *m. violin*

visible, *m. & f. visible*

visita, *f. visit*

visitar, *to visit*

visitas, *f. visitors, company*

vitalidad, *f. vitality*

vitamina, *f. vitamin*

vive, *lives*

vivir, *to live*

vivo, *I live*

voluntaria, *f. voluntary*

voluntario, *m. voluntary*

votar, *to vote*

voy, *I go, I am going*

vuelo, *m. flight, I fly*

Y

y, *and*

yo, *I*

Z

zapatos, *m. (pl.) shoes*

INDEX

CREDITS

p. 45 *Guía del ocio*, Madrid, Spain, No. 84, July 1991. p. 55 *Guía del ocio*, Madrid, Spain, No. 84, July 1991. p. 77 *Pacific Bell*, 1991. p. 144 *En Forma*, Vol. 3, No. 28. p. 157 *Cromos*, No. 3855, December 16, 1991. p. 178 *México desconocido*, Mexico Vol. XVI, No. 185, July 1992. p. 212 *Cruise n' Travel en Español*, Miami, Florida, Independent Publishing Co., Vol. 7, No. 1, 1991. p. 226 *¡Hola!*, No. 2496, June 11, 1992.